No Walk in the Park

Newspapers, Booze and God

Harry Saltzgaver

Saltyman Press

No Walk in the Park
Newspapers, Booze and God
All Rights Reserved.
Copyright © 2026 Harry Saltzgaver
v2.0

The opinions expressed in this manuscript are solely the opinions of the author and do not represent the opinions or thoughts of the publisher. The author has represented and warranted full ownership and/or legal right to publish all the materials in this book.

This book may not be reproduced, transmitted, or stored in whole or in part by any means, including graphic, electronic, or mechanical without the express written consent of the publisher except in the case of brief quotations embodied in critical articles and reviews.

Saltyman Press

ISBN: 979-8-218-80920-1

Cover Photo © 2026 www.gettyimages.com. All rights reserved - used with permission.

PRINTED IN THE UNITED STATES OF AMERICA

"Hey! I ain't finished my testimony."
Harry the Horse in "Guys and Dolls"

Contents

Introduction i
Chapter 1 1
Chapter 2 2
Chapter 3 4
Chapter 4 6
Chapter 5 8
Chapter 6 10
Chapter 7 13
Chapter 8 16
Chapter 9 20
Chapter 10 22
Chapter 11 24
Chapter 12 26
Chapter 13 29
Chapter 14 32
Chapter 15 34
Chapter 16 37
Chapter 17 39
Chapter 18 41
Chapter 19 43
Chapter 20 45
Chapter 21 47

Chapter 22	49
Chapter 23	51
Chapter 24	53
Chapter 25	56
Chapter 26	59
Chapter 27	61
Chapter 28	63
Chapter 29	66
Chapter 30	69
Chapter 31	71
Chapter 32	73
Chapter 33	76
Chapter 34	79
Chapter 35	82
Chapter 36	86
Chapter 37	88
Chapter 38	91
Chapter 39	93
Chapter 40	96
Chapter 41	97
Chapter 42	99
Chapter 43	101
Chapter 44	103
Chapter 45	105
Chapter 46	108
Chapter 47	110

Chapter 48	113
Chapter 49	115
Chapter 50	118
Chapter 51	120
Chapter 52	122
Chapter 53	125
Chapter 54	128
Chapter 55	130
Chapter 56	133
Chapter 57	135
Chapter 58	138
Chapter 59	140
Chapter 60	142
Chapter 61	144
Chapter 62	146
Chapter 63	148
Chapter 64	150
Chapter 65	152
Chapter 66	154
Chapter 67	156
Chapter 68	158
Chapter 69	160
Epilogue	162
Acknowledgements	163

Introduction

Jim and I were driving down the seventh fairway when he asked me.
 "So how did you do it?"
 "It was a God thing," I replied.
 It took the rest of the round of golf to explain those five words to my friend. I'm going to try to explain them to you with this book – and I hope that by the end, you'll be my friend too.
 If nothing else, you'll know why most of my life has been a God thing.
 Jim and I had something in common, and it was more than a love-hate relationship with golf. We are both longtime recovering alcoholics, with more than a taste of various drugs thrown in. We've literally never seen each other outside the environs of a golf course, but we have a shared life experience that binds us together.
 But before we get to the golf course, there's some 40 years of messy living to get through. I'll go fast, I promise.

Chapter 1

Where to begin?

I could start with the time my parents bought me a four-pack of whiskey sours the night before I entered the U.S. Military Academy at West Point in 1971. I was 17, and left the Academy six months later (this was in the middle of the Vietnam War, and Army second lieutenants – your rank when you graduated from West Point – were dropping like flies).

Or I could start with the end of my baseball career in college and the beginning of my serious infatuation with the drug culture of the early 1970s.

Then again, that comparative religions philosophy class in college was impactful – I thought I was a Zen Buddhist for a while.

If you want trauma, there was the time when my first wife said she was leaving with our 18-month-old son because I was "too boring."

In my defense, I'll point out that this was the period when "Real Men" were supposed to eat quiche and be in touch with their feelings. It was the detritus from the Love Child generation. I gravitated towards that kind of stuff.

But I want to make this a story about my "adult" life, so I think it should start when my 40-plus-year career as a newspaper guy began. That way, I can drop in a bit about the rise and demise of journalism in my time, along with the alcoholic story and the spiritual walk.

It's a bit of a roller coaster. Hang on.

Chapter 2

That newspaper career really began a few months after my first wife left. I had been writing a few stories and theater reviews for the weekly newspaper in a little Colorado mountain town called Creede. I worked shifts as a millhand at the silver mine there (the mill is where the silver is separated from the rock).

It took me a few days to wrap my head around the idea of writing full time when Steve offered me the job. On the down side, I'd be cutting my take-home pay by more than 50% – down to $800 a month. On the plus side, I would be making a living using my brain instead of just clocking in for eight-hour shifts of mind-numbing routine (with a toke or two to make the graveyard shifts bearable).

Once I determined that I could make child support payments and buy my beer, I went for it. In 1980, being a reporter was still a glamorous career – it hadn't been that long since Woodward and Bernstein, and the model of living on coffee, cigarettes and Scotch was still being venerated.

Once the career change decision was made, I determined early on to quit smoking marijuana. It really does impact your short-term memory, at least if you've smoked every day for the last seven years, as I had. That left me with beer, Scotch, speed, cocaine, etc., so I figured I could handle it.

A little background might make sense here.

My parents, like many of their peers, were functional alcoholics. By that I mean that they drank every day, but they didn't miss work. They got sloppy occasionally, but rarely fought, and I only saw them get violent twice.

I inherited it all – the addictive personality, the ability to

CHAPTER 2

continue to function and the tendency to be maudlin rather than belligerent. I was pretty convinced that I could indulge and still be better at my job than those around me.

(It should be noted here that most alcoholics think no one around them knows what's really going on, and they are "getting away with it." I can't think of a bigger self-deception.)

Of course I had the advantage of other drugs to supplement my drinking. We had a primitive form of speed we called white crosses – better than caffeine, but they were pills, not methamphetamine to smoke or shoot up. Cocaine was a powder to snort, and too expensive to use unless someone else offered to share.

But a couple of shots of cheap bourbon or scotch could take the edge off at the end of the day, and a few more would allow for a sort of sleep.

God? Religion? It was all a scam, the opiate of the masses, right? I was too smart for that.

Chapter 3

I had pursued several paths in college – four colleges to be technically correct – and ended up with a degree in English Literature, with minors in Philosophy and Biology (I was infatuated with microbiology, at least until I hit organic chemistry). I wrote a lot of papers in those Lit and Philosophy courses, and was told I was a decent writer.

Okay, false humility there. I was told I was a good writer, and should keep it up.

I thought I'd pursue life in the ivory tower of college professorhood, and managed to snag a pretty good graduate fellowship to study overseas when I graduated from a small state college in 1976. That was in Alamosa, in the center of the high mountain desert called the San Luis Valley in south-central Colorado. The wife wasn't too crazy about living in another country, but agreed as long as we could spend the summer in the mountain town of Creede (where her best friend lived) about 70 miles to the west while I found the right university to pursue.

It was the mid-1970s and we were dirt poor, but that didn't stop us from having a stash of pot. I discovered the bars where the silver miners hung out for my "me" time – Creede is so small stumbling home was no issue.

It took a couple of months for me to get a real job at the local sawmill. It also took about that long for Oxford to inform me I wasn't quite their cup of tea.

So instead of the long-term motel we had been staying in, we rented a little house, and I started researching alternatives. Australia? New Zealand?

By that time, it was getting close to winter – the Southern

CHAPTER 3

Hemisphere was no longer feasible. How about Wales the following year?

Funny how your mind works when you're stoned. Hey, maybe that's why they call it being stoned!

I had lots of those Eureka moments back then.

It was clear we were in Creede for a year, and I managed to get a job with the Homestake Mining Company – the biggest reason Creede was still a town. It was shift work in the silver mill, but it paid pretty well.

And Creede did have a bit of culture. A group of theater students from the University of Kansas had discovered the Colorado mountains a generation or so ago, and established the Creede Repertory Theatre. The English Lit thing included Shakespeare and some more modern theatrical writing, so I convinced the owners of a little weekly called the *Mineral County Miner* that I could write reviews for them.

It paid $10 or $15 (about the price of a lid, or ounce, of pot back then) and kept me writing, so it seemed like a good deal for all involved.

About the *Mineral County Miner*. This was a true mom and pop operation, owned by a couple who pretty much did it all themselves. They sold the paper for a quarter in news boxes and at the town's one grocery store, along with some mail subscriptions. That store's weekly advertisement pretty much paid the bills – the mailed circulation surely didn't. The population was around 650, with maybe 400 more living within 20 miles or so.

I typed my reviews on an electric portable typewriter, using *Liquid Paper* (love that name) to make corrections. I later reverted to a Remington manual when the portable died.

I handed the two or three pages in, and let the O'Rourkes do their magic. I had no idea how a paper got produced, but it got done. And my review was right there, with my name at the top and everything.

And I got toasted, smoking with the wife and drinking alone.

Chapter 4

God and circumstance put an end to the grad school pipe dream in the form of a pregnancy – who eventually became Alexander Cox Saltzgaver in February 1979. I wasn't aware at the time that God was involved, of course, but you know He was.

Actually, I sort of thought it was a plot by the wife. When she told me she was pregnant, that was followed almost immediately by "and I'm not having a baby overseas."

Goodbye fellowship.

To be honest, I was relieved. I had begun to think I wasn't good enough to keep my head above water in any foreign land, let alone complete a graduate program successfully.

And I did like the idea of being a dad.

There also was news on the newspaper front. The kind, but elderly, couple who owned the paper decided to retire. Thankfully, instead of shutting down they sold the *Mineral County Miner* to a youngish couple from Kansas.

Steve Haynes had spent the last 11 years at the *Kansas City Times*. But he and his wife Cynthia wanted to bring their children up in a rural setting, and had been to Creede before on vacation. Serendipity.

Apparently, he thought my reviews read pretty well, and he needed some writing help if he was going to turn the family weekly into a real newspaper (I loved the O'Rourkes, but well…). So he asked me to expand into doing a little hard news.

He probably second guessed that decision when I turned in the first story about a Mineral County Supervisors meeting. I started with a roll call, then provided a chronological account of the proceedings.

CHAPTER 4

Steve was patient and, aware that there weren't too many people with typewriters in Creede, began teaching me the craft of newspaper writing. I was fascinated. It didn't take long to drop the English Lit term paper approach.

This was long before the days of miniature recorders, and I was happy with the cool reporter's notebook that slid into my back pocket. I came up with my own version of shorthand so I could keep up at meetings and interviews – and no one else could make heads or tails of my notes.

By this time, Alex had arrived and we had a bit of a family routine. Steve even hired the wife part-time as a typesetter. This wasn't cold type, but typing on a machine that would develop strips of copy in the proper column width. It was called phototypesetting, and the result was literally a strip of photo paper with words developed on it.

This was a sort of intermediate evolution from actual cold type typesetting to computer-generated copy. I'll mention this continued evolution as we go along – it parallels the evolution of computers themselves.

I sort of watched the paste-up process, but didn't really get involved at the time. Hey, I was the reporter and photographer – much too important to do that stuff.

Besides, I had to get to the bar after turning in a story.

Chapter 5

It felt like someone pulled the rug out from under me, and there was a 10-foot-deep hole under the rug.

I know there are far too many people who have suffered a separation and divorce, but when it happens to you (me) it feels like no one has ever felt so bad. And it's really, really unfair.

As I said before, the immediate claim was that I was "boring." Her actions made it clear that "boring" included sex. That does something to the ego, if you know what I mean.

With the benefit of 40 years of hindsight, I am sure the fact I was drunk and/or high most of the time really did make me boring. That didn't dawn on me then, however. And hey, I was bringing a paycheck home, wasn't I?

By that time we were living in a pretty big house, thanks to the inlaws (another little ego deflator). I started sleeping in the spare bedroom, and we avoided each other while she tried to figure out how she could get away from me.

That only lasted a few painful months. I remember we had a second birthday for Alex in that house. I was there, but I felt like an outsider.

Remember I said the alcoholic gene in my family was not violent. I never touched her, and I don't remember ever yelling. It was all very civilized. At least the part that I can remember.

This type of drama is a fine excuse to drown your sorrows, and I took every opportunity to do just that.

One thing I didn't do is try to fix whatever was wrong. This was the 1980s, when divorce was almost expected, and certainly easy. We'd been married for 7 years – that was a good run in those days.

CHAPTER 5

So it was easier to go with the flow. I still had the occasional writing assignment to get done before I could start drinking, and I couldn't miss a shift at the mine – bills still had to be paid.

Have you ever carried a six-pack of beer on a mountain hike at 9,000 feet? I have. I had to get away, and couldn't afford a pint of whiskey.

But somehow, I always made it back to town. One foot in front of the other, you know.

The limbo finally ended when she found a job working for a lawyer back in Alamosa, where we had gone to college. That came in handy – she was able to type up the divorce papers herself, so it didn't cost as much.

She made the 70-mile move, and I got myself out of the house. I actually lived in a real cave set up as a bedroom by some friends for a while, and then a little single-wide trailer. That trailer smelled like burnt TV dinner – I passed out more than once with one still in the oven.

As you can tell, I was pretty miserable. I got to see Alex every other weekend, meeting them halfway to make the exchange. I was careful to be sober when I went to get him and managed to hold it down to a beer or three while he was around.

We went to the school playground, watched TV, walked around – entertaining a toddler can be a chore in a small mountain town.

You'd think that someone who had a philosophy degree (at least a minor) might have looked for a way to change the situation – maybe even look for a Higher Power. Not me, not then. I took solace in the bottle.

After all, none of it was my fault. I was the victim here, and there wasn't anything I could do about it. So I just waited for something to change.

Chapter 6

When do you know you're starting the rest of your life? At least in my experience, it's certainly not when you start the rest of your life.

It takes a few years, is what I'm trying to say. I certainly knew when my life physically changed, which it did with considerable regularity in my 20s and 30s. But I didn't know this next one would shape the entire future.

The big change came when Steve decided he wanted to expand the newspaper operation. We had begun delivering papers in a non-incorporated area about 20 miles downstream from Creede called South Fork – it was where the south fork of the Rio Grande met up with the main river. He had this idea to produce a second paper, called the *South Fork Tines* (fork tines, get it?), a play on the common newspaper name of *Times*.

At any rate, he sat me down and said I ought to think about journalism as a career. It was clear that type of work suited me far better than mining/milling. He even had me apply at another paper in Kansas and take an interview, just to see that the job offer wasn't a charity thing for a guy going through a divorce.

There was a definite down side – he couldn't or wouldn't offer me more than $800 a month (I was bringing home more than $1,600 from the silver mine). This was 1980, but that still wasn't much. And I had promised to pay $200 a month in child support.

Still, for some strange reason, he thought I could do the job.

I'm not sure what he saw in me. I know I enjoyed writing, I took pride in being in the paper. I'd always been a quick study, and he was a good editor/teacher, so the product was adequate – maybe better than that.

I took it. Steve had found me a cheap place to rent in South

CHAPTER 6

Fork, and a room that could be turned into a newspaper office. I had a job offer from the Kansas paper, but South Fork was 50 miles away from Alex, not 300.

For most of a year, we published a paper we called the *Mineral County Miner & South Fork Tines*, with a page or two inside for the Tines. Then, on Dec. 3, 1981, we published the first separate *South Fork Tines*.

It didn't take much physically – the idea was to make two front pages so Creede and South Fork would each have their own paper. We switched stories on an inside page too, with the opposite town's news. But the bulk of the content, and the pages, were the same. We gradually started changing other components, but we were a very small staff – I was the only editorial hired hand – and saving labor was important.

I learned a vital newspaper lesson from Steve here. If you want a town to call a paper its own, you damn well better have a staff person living there. You have to be part of the community to call yourself a community newspaper.

The enforced poverty did my health a little good, too. I had quit smoking marijuana, both because of the cost and what it did to my memory. I sure couldn't pay for any other types of drugs.

I couldn't afford to go to the bar every night – I could still get a six-pack of beer for around two bucks when it was on sale, though. A fifth of cheap whiskey was $3. And I was going to cut back. Honest.

No, I didn't pray about the decision. I still thought little about God, at least a Christian God, I had no concept of a Higher Power. I had a vague idea about some overarching whole (Baba Ram Dass was big back then), but that was about it. A majority of my generation felt the same.

It would be a good 20 years before I realized that was the first time God really hit me on the head with a 2x4 and changed my life's direction (maybe the second – leaving West Point was a pretty big change, too).

◄ NO WALK IN THE PARK

I knew pretty quickly I'd done the right thing. Facing dropping silver prices, the Homestake Mining Company essentially stopped operations six months after I left, and laid almost everyone off.

It was a big story.

Chapter 7

It was time to learn the business. We were a small, really small, outfit and didn't have what you'd call state-of-the-art equipment. I had graduated from the Remington typewriter to a first-generation computer. But I typed everything in – my stories, the society column from the nice lady who'd been doing it for years, the occasional letter – then transferred it to a floppy disk. That was the first generation of external, portable data storage.

Steve and I met halfway between our two towns, then he'd take my stuff back to Creede and edit it before giving it to his wife, Cynthia, (a part-timer took over soon) to phototypeset. Steve had a darkroom and developed the photographic paper and our photographs (black and white only).

Then on Wednesday night I'd go up to Creede and we'd put the paper together. It's exactly what it sounds like – we'd trim the copy into columns and paste it onto full-sized cardboard grid boards. That included headlines, pictures and captions, even advertisements.

Have you heard the phrase ending up on the cutting room floor? I know there's a movie editing version, but that's also how we managed to make stories fit exactly on pages – cutting the copy with an exacto knife, with what was cut ending up on the floor. It is a lost art.

The idea is that you would end up with a complete page. Once you had 16, 20 or 24 of those, you had a newspaper.

Those pages went to the printing plant – the one we used was 60 some miles away – the next morning and they took a picture of each page with something called a PMT (Photo Mechanical Transfer) camera. Those negatives were used to burn plates that went onto the printing press. The whole thing was called off-set printing and it was actually pretty cool. Time consuming, but cool.

I managed to handle the mechanical stuff, but I was much more interested in the reporting side. I was clearly still very green, and made plenty of mistakes.

I still remember covering the first South Fork Chamber of Commerce meeting. I just joined in the discussion, and wasn't apprised of my proper place until I tried to vote on something. "You're a reporter, stupid! You don't vote!"

But I got to talk to some very interesting people, and do some really cool things. South Fork is a near paradise for nature types – the stretch of the Rio Grande River between Creede and South Fork is a Gold Medal trout stream, there are two wilderness areas in the surrounding mountains and the town is at the base of Wolf Creek Pass.

"Wolf Creek Pass, Way up on the Great Divide, Truckin' on down the other side" was a big hit back then for a singer named C.W. McCall. The two-lane pass reaches nearly 11,000 feet and is famous for its switchbacks and hairpin turns.

I got to ride with a snowplow driver on that pass during a storm. The Wolf Creek Ski Area wasn't fancy, but it was near the summit, and was famous for regularly getting the most snow in the state. Steve got me an annual pass so I could take pictures.

That pass and the surrounding wilderness gave me a couple of stories that won a few awards, too.

I thought I was settling in pretty well. I wasn't really making any friends, but that seemed okay. I spent most of my spare time alone, drinking beer and watching TV, in between Alex visits.

I still hung out in Creede from time to time, thanks to the theater and the Old Miners Inn. That's the bar where I'd celebrate with a Scotch or three once the paper had been put together before I made the drive back to South Fork.

Did I mention that the road between Creede and South Fork, State Highway 149, is mostly on a cliff above the river? Two lanes,

CHAPTER 7

with very little shoulder and one of those 3-foot-tall guardrails in a few sections – nothing but air in other places.

Let's just say I didn't have one of those "God is my copilot" bumper stickers. But apparently He was exactly that. I made it home every time.

Chapter 8

Being the only news source in a couple hundred square miles can be a daunting task. Oh, there was a daily newspaper in Alamosa, but they rarely headed to our side of the valley, let alone into the San Juan Mountains to get to Creede.

Early on, it could be a struggle to find enough "news" to fill the two pages dedicated to South Fork news, much less the inside pages where the territory stretched from Creede to at least the middle of the San Luis Valley. We'd write about literally everything. I did mention we had a very popular society columnist, didn't I?

The longer I was in the job, the easier it was to find news, though. That was true at every paper I've ever worked for, by the way. And the issues are much the same if there are 200 residents or 200,000.

Back then, the South Fork Sewer Board was the only elected agency in the unincorporated town. The intrigue and shenanigans were taken just as seriously as they were at the big city councils I later covered. The big difference was that in South Fork or Creede you'd have to look whoever you had written about that week in the eye at the grocery store when the paper came out.

Remember, this was the early 1980s. Telephones still had wires. Cars had carburetors. I had the latest in technology though – a police scanner. The thing was supposed to be by my side and on 24/7. I didn't take it into the bar, though.

The scanner paid off multiple times, occasionally getting me to news scenes before the cops or the ambulance got there. That could prove awkward, but I knew most of the officers and EMTs pretty well.

One summer day in 1983, there was a call about a couple of

CHAPTER 8

guys waving guns as they drove through Del Norte, the town just east of South Fork. I hustled out to the highway where one trooper had the car stopped and was in place before the second trooper got on scene.

The picture of him with a gun drawn covering one man while his partner handcuffed the second one took second place nationally in the news photo contest that year.

I even left the thing on at night, a habit that got me one of the biggest stories of my early career – maybe my entire career.

The call came in pretty late at night – a tractor-trailer had slid off the road going up the pass. No big deal, that happened a few times each year.

But the follow-up call was for the volunteer fire department and search and rescue. The big truck had a family in the cab. It had been pushed off the road by an avalanche and down a 100-foot slope.

The pass was still icy in May, but I had chains for my little truck, so off I went. Twenty minutes later I was parked 100 yards or so below a group of big trucks, a snowbank and a lot of lights.

By the time I got to the scene, someone had made it down to the truck cab. Two adults, two kids, he radioed to the command post. I heard it, and it wasn't good.

A baby was missing (her body was found the next day) and both parents were dead. A 2-year-old girl was alive, though.

I had been busily taking pictures, trying to conserve the one roll of film I had with me. But then the volunteers rushed to the rope attached to the EMT and started pulling. "We need more help here!"

The rescuer had the little girl and they were bringing them up. I stashed the camera and grabbed the rope.

One of the first rules of reporting is to tell the story, don't be the story. I wasn't the story that night, but I did have a small part in it. And the long story about my experience eventually won a first place national award for breaking news in 1983.

Of course, I had two days to write that story, and Steve had

NO WALK IN THE PARK

time to edit it. There was no rush to get something up online. And while the Alamosa and Pueblo papers had the basics (three dead, one survived), I was the only one with a first-person account.

That pressure to be the first to put something online is a huge part of what's wrong with journalism today compared to then. And I mentioned I had an editor, right? For most websites these days, that's the exception, not the rule.

But I digress. Back to South Fork.

After the rescue, things went back to normal. In the mountains, that's what you did when stuff like that happened. You dealt with it and you moved on. I was beginning to accept that style too.

Over the five years I was the managing editor at South Fork, I spent three days on horseback with a search party looking for a lost bow hunter in the Weminuche Wilderness; waited for the coroner beside the body of a girl in the woods two weeks after I had talked to her parents about their missing daughter; got charged by a bull while taking pictures at a Little Britches Rodeo; fell out of an innertube during a raft race down the Rio Grande and barely survived; flew in a helicopter counting elk, and interviewed some of the most amazing people I've ever met.

The hunter wasn't found (dead in a creek) until I had made it back to South Fork. I had to interview the parents again after they were told their daughter died. The bull was as young as the young rodeo participants, but I was in the arena and he chased me up the fence. And so on.

I also raised a few thousand bucks for the Creede Repertory Theatre in two ski marathons at the Wolf Creek Ski Area, and wrote reviews of their plays for the entire time I was there. I still treasure a framed season poster from CRT hanging in my living room.

That's just what I can remember 40 years later. And my memory wasn't the best back then.

I would celebrate a good day and mourn a bad day much the same way. It didn't matter if all I had to eat were a couple fried potatoes, I had my drink to put me to sleep.

THE SOUTH FORK TIMES

25¢

Two Sections, 28 Pages

South Fork, Colorado 81154

Thursday, May 5, 1983

'3' sweep school vote in Del Norte

Perley wins against two opponents to shift control

By Harry Saltzgaver and Brenda Denney

Perley of South Fork, outdistanced an incumbent and another South Fork man for a two-year seat on the South Fork school board Tuesday, giving control of the board to a coalition which says the district needs change.

Dan Davey and Jay Schrader were the winners for the four-year seats, gathering more than twice the number of votes Rita Roybal or Mary Talley received. They and Mr. Perley campaigned together on a ticket that urged change.

More than 1,300 people, a record, cast ballots in the heated election.

Perley beat Alyse Dominguez, incumbent, by 28 votes in Del Norte, and received almost 200 more votes than Terrell, the other two-year candidate.

Continued on Page 16A

New board will get hire principals

New members of the Del Norte school board will have a hand in hiring new and high school principals despite a delay in interviewing candidates.

Dominguez, who was running for re-election, and hold-over member Terrell had pushed to hire at least one principal before the new board was seated. Carl Perley, a board member running against Mrs. Dominguez, and other candidates had asked the hiring be delayed until the newly elected members were on the board.

President James Beck said last week, with recommendations ready at the meeting Thursday night, voting Mr. Beck said that interviews was ready, but the

Continued on Page 16A

Mark Hoffman of South Fork makes ready to secure the trailer wrapped around a rock spire, which had to be anchored before searchers could look in the ravine below for a 4-week-old baby thrown from the tractor. Sgt. Chauncy Clark of the State Patrol (lower right) holds a flashlight and offers advice. (Staff photo by Steve Haynes)

'Miracle' saves tot as family dies on pass

Searchers work through long, windy night to find missing baby

Three members of a Texas family were killed last week when their tractor-trailer rig crashed through the overlook guardrail on the west side of Wolf Creek Pass at 70 miles an hour and plunged 1,300 feet to the bottom of the cliff.

A 2-year-old girl survived the crash and more than 40 rescuers searched all night for her 4-week-old brother, only to find him dead early Thursday morning.

The truck went down a steep ravine and Mark and Lew Hoffman, owners of Climb & Glide Mountaineering in South Fork, were called to help. They and Bob Bernard completed a difficult maneuver to secure the trailer, which was hanging from a rock pinnacle. The South Fork Fire Department provided its searchlights and generator.

Rick Donner and Dave Donaldson, state troopers from South Fork, went over the edge on ropes during the search and Mr. Donaldson spent almost two hours between the truck and trailer, directing searchers below.

The driver, Danny K. Vaughan, 25, Earth, Texas, was westbound down U.S. 160 on the west side of Wolf Creek Pass about 7:30 p.m. April 27 when his truck went out of control. State Trooper Larry Pool of Pagosa Springs said that Mr. Vaughan's truck missed the runaway ramp above Lobo Overlook, skidded and turned onto its side before going through the guardrail.

Mr. Vaughan was travelling with his wife Sharla, 24, daughter Amber, 2, and son Adam, 4 weeks. The couple and the baby died of massive head injuries after being thrown from the truck. The daughter survived, suffering a broken collar-

Continued on Page 9A

Motel, shopping center planned for McClung land

Construction of a 50-unit motel, scheduled to begin this month, is just the first phase of a development plan for South Fork that includes a larger motel, two restaurants, a bank or savings and loan, a shopping center and condominiums, the Oklahoma men responsible say.

Frank Wright, Piedmont, and Ken Sutton, Stillwater, have formed the S & W Development Partnership and are working with L. B. McClung to develop land on both sides of U.S. 160 in west South Fork. Construction of the Wolf Creek Ski Lodge, between the Powder Connection Ski and Gift Shop and the Westique Village, will start before June 1, Mr. Wright said, with the rest of the development coming as it is needed.

"It will be a phased development," Mr. Wright said. "We're looking at doing it within the next three years. We hope to have this motel complete by Nov. 22. I plan to have busloads of people from Oklahoma and Dallas there for Thanksgiving weekend."

Mr. Wright said he is president of Homewood Corp. in Oklahoma City, a residential developer with more than 900 houses under construction.

Mr. Sutton owns Sutton Construction Co. in Stillwater. He will be the builder and manager in the South Fork partner-

Continued on Page 16A

Chapter 9

About that drink. As I said, I was a functional alcoholic, and didn't drink during the day (most of the time). I'd have some pretty good hangovers, but tried hard to avoid the hair-of-the-dog remedy.

My work ethic was strong, and my pride in that work was strong as well. Both were more than enough to get the job done before I celebrated the end of the day.

It was tougher on the weekend. I'd try to take some time for myself, only to get pulled back into covering a story when something unexpected happened. I had to do that with the smell of alcohol on my breath more than once.

I got better at the job, faster with my writing. Organizing stories came pretty naturally to me, and I was blessed with the ability to write cleanly, so there wasn't too much backing up and fixing things.

And I was an early riser, even after a night of drinking. That was ingrained in my metabolism back in college, when I did a stint as the baker at Al's Bakery in Alamosa – starting at 4 a.m. six days a week before classes.

So I could normally say the day was done and the drinking begun as the sun went down. There were a few Fridays where I'd even make the drive to Alamosa to find some fun when it wasn't my weekend to have Alex.

A couple of years in, the wonder of telephone modems arrived, and I was able to transmit stories instead of physically meeting up with Steve. That was one less chance to get myself in trouble.

Unfortunately, the longer you get away with something without serious trouble, the more you push the boundaries. I started drinking more. I thought I was picking my spots and no one was

CHAPTER 9

noticing, but in hindsight I know that wasn't true.

One of those spots where I was sure it was safe to have a drink or two came weekly, after we had put the paper to bed – finished putting the pages together and in the box for transport. We did that work in Creede, and it was an all hands on deck thing to get it done before midnight.

I had worked hard all week, so I deserved a drink, right? The Old Miners Inn stayed open late even on weekdays, and I was a regular.

It started out fine. A couple of drinks and I'd hit the road. Twenty miles of curves above the Rio Grande late at night, but there was seldom any traffic on either lane, so it wasn't too hard to make it back to South Fork.

Only after a couple of years, I'd leave Creede and the next thing I knew I'd be in South Fork. No memory of the drive.

That's called a blackout, for those of you unfamiliar with the life of an alcoholic. I was so drunk I didn't have a memory of what I had done for a period of time.

Blackouts can be embarrassing if you are around other people. They can be dangerous, even deadly, as well.

I still have no clue why I hadn't driven off the cliff into the river. But that didn't stop me from doing it again. And again.

Today I have no doubt that God was keeping me alive for a higher purpose. That comes later, though. Much later.

Chapter 10

It was really only a matter of time before it happened.

I don't remember what led up to it. All I know is that it was winter, I got to drinking, and decided it would be a good idea to drive to Alamosa to visit a girl, even though it was snowing.

You know what's coming, right?

I hit a patch of ice and slid off the side of the road into a snow-filled ditch. It wasn't very late, but there wasn't much traffic on the road – not too many folks willing to chance the bad weather, I guess.

So I just sat there, waiting to sober up enough to try to get out of the ditch. I wasn't really surprised when the blue and red lights came on behind me.

I knew the state trooper who walked up to the window, and he knew me. That didn't stop him from arresting me, and taking me down to the county jail in the next town – Del Norte by name. I spent the night behind bars there.

They let me out on my own recognizance the next morning. Steve's sister came down to give me a ride home.

The embarrassment – from talking to the state trooper to pleading with Steve for forgiveness – was as painful as anything else. Drinking and driving wasn't the social anathema it is today, but getting caught sure was.

I had to promise I'd only drive to and from work (they didn't automatically take your license away in those days) and waited for the trial. In another consequence of living in a small town, the judge was a lawyer friend who happened to own a restaurant/bar in South Fork that I had frequented on occasion.

Just like the state trooper, the judge did his duty. I kept a restricted license, but was ordered to start taking Antabuse, a drug

CHAPTER 10

designed to make you deathly ill if you drank alcohol.

Was I repentant? Not really. I was more resentful. I didn't deserve this, dammit.

I was also stubborn, or rather my addiction was stubborn. After a couple of months, I found myself on a barstool, even though I had been taking the Antabuse as required.

I found out that I could indeed drink a beer without dying. It didn't feel all that good, but ... another month and the pills stayed on the shelf while I went back to my old habits.

At least I did until I put a serious dent in the company truck.

It was one of those little Datsun pickups. I was driving it home from a girl's house after a drink or three. Winter again, with plenty of snow and ice.

I pulled into the parking space next to my cabin, and slid right into the side of the building.

I would argue that could have happened if I had been stone-cold sober — in fact, I believe I did just that. But I was still on probation, so to speak, and this time it was company property.

Steve said there was only one way I could keep my job. I had to join AA.

Chapter 11

South Fork wasn't very big, but it was big enough to have an Alcoholics Anonymous chapter. The hosts, a fairly well-to-do couple from Texas, welcomed me. The guy, I'll call him Bill, told me he was my sponsor and I had to do what he said.

I say again that the job and the newspaper had become pretty much the most important things in my life by this time – except for Alex, maybe the only thing. So I did as I was told.

Once I got over the physical withdrawals, the lack of alcohol only had one immediate impact. I had a tough, tough time getting to sleep.

That was partly due to AA, too. You see, one of the big parts about the Twelve Steps of Recovery is to take a personal inventory. That includes recalling all the bad things you had done. The emphasis was on the stuff you did under the influence, but once I started down that road it quickly became a review of all the failures and perceived slights given and received over my life.

It was depressing. My parents, God rest their souls, motivated through guilt, so I learned early on just how bad I was and how hard it would be to overcome that bad.

The answer, a Power Higher Than Me, was in front of my face. From the Big Book:

"Step 2: Came to believe that a Power greater than ourselves could restore us to sanity. Step 3: Made a decision to turn our will and our lives over to the care of God as we understood Him."

God was there, no doubt. But I fought giving my life over to Him tooth and nail, getting into some silly (serious at the time though) arguments about defining God, giving up control, etc. I just wasn't going to accept this God everyone else kept talking

CHAPTER 11

about with absolutely no proof.

I finally compromised by admitting that there was some sort of higher power, even if I didn't know what it was or how I could reach it. I struggled with admitting that I was powerless over alcohol, the first half of the first step, but I had pretty good proof of the truth of the second half of the same step – my life had become unmanageable.

So I went to a meeting a week, and Bill sometimes took me to a second meeting somewhere else in the Valley. For the first few months, I went back on Antabuse as a sort of safety net.

I strung together a whole year of sobriety. When I got that 1-year chip, I thought I had it licked.

Note that I said I – clearly my own strength of willpower was the reason I had made it. Not a higher power, not a program. Me.

That, my friends, is a recipe for failure. But I didn't know that then.

Chapter 12

During this period, the newspapers thrived. Circulation of both the *Mineral County Miner* and the *South Fork Tines* increased, and we were collecting more awards each year in the Colorado Press Association's Better Newspapers Contest. Various special promotional sections made the company more profitable.

Those awards probably had a lot to do with Steve's increasing involvement in the CPA board, but naturally I thought it was all about my amazing talent in writing and taking pictures. There's nothing quite like the ego of a young hotshot, and that was me.

Let me talk a bit about newspapers in general in the early- to mid-1980s, and the place of the rural community newspaper in particular.

There were, of course, the major television networks and their powerhouse news departments. The Vietnam War had shown the impact of live television coverage in the 1970s, and Walter Cronkite single-handedly showed how a national audience could change government policy.

Cronkite took a trip to Vietnam in 1968, and when he returned, he trashed the U.S.'s involvement, arguing that it was a war we couldn't win. That broadcast is widely acknowledged as the reason Lyndon B. Johnson declined to run for another term as president.

In the 1980s, newspapers still held sway as the arbiters of truth. National papers like the *Wall Street Journal*, the *New York Times* and the *Washington Post* told us all what was important on the world and national stages. And their credibility was essentially unquestioned.

Regional and daily municipal newspapers filled the same role in their bailiwicks, with the emphasis on the more local news – state and city politics, business developments, sports, etc. In Colorado,

CHAPTER 12

the *Denver Post* and the *Rocky Mountain News* were considered statewide papers, and were distributed all across the state from their Denver bases.

The cities and towns all had papers of their own – the bigger the city, the bigger the paper. And in a state like Colorado where television was controlled by one city, the newspapers dictated what was local news and what wasn't worth the ink.

That's why rural weeklies were so important. I mentioned that the Alamosa paper wasn't going to travel to the mountains often to cover the goings-on in Creede. It's a good bet that the Denver television station managers didn't even know where Creede was.

But the people who live in and around those towns are much more interested in what their neighbors are doing than what the state legislature is up to (except when it directly impacts them). News about the health of the sawmill or the price of wheat means more to daily lives than the national unemployment rate or the state's infrastructure budget.

That's why, 10 years down the road, I would come back to community weeklies. I thought that niche would never go away.

Two more things about newspapers in the 1980s and 1990s. First, most were locally owned. If there was a chain, it was a small one.

Second, they were profitable thanks to advertising sales. Sure, subscriptions brought some money in, but the size of circulation was really important primarily when it came to the ads. The number of readers determined the price ads could be sold for, and why business owners should buy them.

That advertising was a service provided by newspapers, too, particularly in rural areas. That's where people looked when they needed to buy something, from a home to a used bicycle. People found jobs in the classified ads, because that's where businesses advertised job openings. And display ads were where business owners let potential customers know there was a reason to visit the store.

NO WALK IN THE PARK

Then the Internet went public. But I'm getting ahead of myself here.

Technology was advancing in the early '80s, but slowly. Computers were making it easier to write, and to prepare the material that went on the page.

But we still had to put the physical pages together, and I still made the drive to Salida every week, across the valley floor and over Poncha Pass.

I discovered that the drive was much more pleasant when I didn't have a hangover.

Chapter 13

It was about this time that a woman I had known in high school, then in college, resurfaced.

To be honest, I don't remember exactly how or when it became a relationship. We started seeing each other occasionally – she lived in Pueblo, a good 170 miles from South Fork – typically with her visiting me.

Eventually we took a cross-country road trip that included a blowup over me not being willing to take extra days away from work to be with her. That mindset of putting work first stayed with me for decades.

Clearly, she was dead set on marriage. I suspect it was a biological clock thing – we were both past 30. Bottom line, she asked, and I said yes.

Why did I do that? I can't claim I was drunk – this was my first long sober phase.

I had known her and her family for more than a decade. It's fair to say we were close. But there was no great romance, and in retrospect very little love.

I will say I had been lonely for quite some time. There had been a few casual hookups, but mostly when I was drinking. I was floundering when it came to companionship, no doubt.

There was the newspaper situation as well. We were on a roll, with growing circulation and advertising sales for both Creede and South Fork, and the kudos kept coming in.

I remained the only full-time editorial employee, if you don't count Steve's dual role of executive editor and publisher in charge of sales. We had some valuable contributors, to be sure.

But I was certain that our success was directly attributable to my talents as a writer, photographer, etc. In a delusional self-deception of grandeur and total lack of understanding of business, I actually expected Steve and Cynthia to give me part ownership of the papers (after just more than three years working full time). Seriously. Even I can't believe that.

I think Steve might have given me a raise. But he properly dismissed my ownership request out of hand.

I say that in hindsight. I really did think I deserved it back then. I might have been in what we call a dry drunk — losing contact with reality even though you are sober; I don't know how else I could have ignored reality so completely.

At any rate, it felt like life was telling me it was time for a change. And here was that marriage thing.

She had a good job in Pueblo with the school district there — no way was she going to give that up. I had graduated high school in Pueblo and knew the town.

And I was the greatest thing to hit journalism since Bob Woodward of Watergate fame, so it would be no problem to convince the paper there to give me a job, right? (Did I mention the concept of a dry drunk?)

There was the issue of leaving my South Fork AA group. But Pueblo was a big city, at least comparatively, and I could find another group.

Famous last words.

Steve and Cynthia were gracious. They probably knew I was nuts, but I don't remember them trying to talk me out of it. I didn't have another job lined up. But I turned in my resignation anyway. They still came to the wedding!

We had already submitted entries for the next Better Newspapers Contest. My last full year there, the *South Fork Tines* was named the best small weekly newspaper in the state.

But I was gone. I borrowed the money for the big church wedding she wanted, packed my trunk and headed to Pueblo.

CHAPTER 13

I wish I could say I was leaving it in the hands of God — and He most definitely was making moves with an eye on my distant future — but I still wasn't a believer.

In the vernacular of the day, I was just going with the flow.

Chapter 14

It turned out that I wasn't quite the superstar I thought I was. The Denver and Colorado Springs dailies didn't have any interest, and the *Pueblo Chieftain* hemmed and hawed, finally saying they didn't have an open position.

I expanded my job search, adding a little humble pie to the resume.

In the meantime, I dawdled in my effort to find a new AA home. I tried a couple of groups, but they weren't a "fit," at least according to me.

Looking back, it seems pretty clear I was just looking for a reason to slip back into my alcoholic ways. I was out from under the weekly commitment to the South Fork group, and wife two really had no buy-in either way. In short, there was no one keeping me accountable.

I honestly don't remember the first drink of this next round. It probably was a stop at a sports bar to watch a game.

I kept things under control; just a beer here and there to "take the edge off." But I don't wait well, and the longer I didn't have a job, the edgier I got.

Then I caught a break. The *Greeley Tribune* called and asked if I could come up for an interview.

Back then, Greeley's claim to fame was the Monfort Beef Packing Plant. The town is about 60 miles north of Denver, and is the county seat of Weld County. Weld is farm country, and the Tribune is the only daily newspaper in the county.

And yes, it and the town are named after Horace Greeley, a newspaper owner/editor now known best for the phrase "Go West, young man." He never made it to Greeley during his one

CHAPTER 14

stagecoach trip west, although he did visit Denver before returning to New York City.

It turns out that the Tribune's editorial page editor, Ed Ott, had been a Better Newspapers Contest judge for the last couple of years, and recognized my name. The interview went well.

The money offered wasn't much, but it was significantly more than a weekly editor could make. There was just one issue.

Greeley is 175 miles from Pueblo.

But it had been two months since I had brought in a paycheck. Wife two was quick to agree with me moving to Greeley, returning to Pueblo on weekends. That drive was a straight shot down Interstate 25 through Denver and Colorado Springs.

A week later, I was the new cop reporter for the *Greeley Tribune*, happy as a clam.

And I had my own apartment again, with no one to watch me when I wasn't working…

Chapter 15

Greeley had a reputation for being a smelly cow town, and truth be told, the air could get ripe if the wind was blowing the right way off the packing plant. But I discovered that it wasn't a bad little city.

There was both a community college and a small university. There were a couple of high schools, and the smaller schools in the surrounding small towns played a high level of baseball.

The *Tribune* was a pretty good small daily paper. It used some nationally-produced wire stories to fill space, but focused on local and regional issues. There were half a dozen reporters in the newsroom, and they had a sports department, too.

As was the case with most dailies back in the 1980s, the *Tribune* had its own printing press. So the whole process was self-contained – ads sold and created by the staff, pages physically pasted up by graphic artists, presses run, delivery trucks loaded.

We moved to a brand-new building my first year there, and we had to start going outside to smoke. That was a bit of a pain, but having a new mainframe computer – we each had our own terminal – made it all worthwhile.

At the time, mainframe computers were the top-of-the-line technology. Housed in a separate climate-controlled room, the giant computer could handle multiple tasks at once, fed by terminals wired into it. Work spaces consisted of a screen and a keyboard.

It was a true disaster when the main frame decided to shut down, typically losing all the work being done at the time.

I really enjoyed learning to be a daily reporter. I thrived on the quick turnaround of making a daily deadline with a story, and my

CHAPTER 15

police- and ambulance-chasing experience in South Fork stood me in good stead.

There were some good editors to work with too. Admittedly, it was hard for me to hear that my work could actually be improved. But I learned the lessons quickly.

I found that one of Steve's journalistic edicts worked really well when dealing with what was, for me, the big city cops and bureaucrats. I met with them early and promised to write positive stories as long as they understood that when there was bad news, I'd write about that, too – and that they would talk to me about it. That way, readers would know I was telling the truth, good or bad.

I leaned on that approach to establishing credibility for my entire career.

It wasn't long, maybe six months or so, before I was promoted to the city hall beat. I'd been a closet political wonk most of my adult life, and quickly took to that beat. I found I could write stories every day – there's nothing like a daily byline to feed the ego.

It turns out that one of God's many blessings to me is an ability to explain complex subjects like city budgets in an understandable way. I took full advantage of that.

On the personal side of things, I wasn't progressing so well. The trips to Pueblo weren't too bad, at least at first, and getting together with wife two just a couple days a week made it easier for both of us, I think.

She talked me into buying a motorcycle – she bought one too and we actually went on a few rides together. I kept that motorcycle for more than 20 years, and loved almost every minute of it.

Her dad helped us buy a large single-wide mobile home. I think they call them modular homes these days. That gave us something to work on during the weekend visits too.

But during the week, I lived by myself in Greeley.

I had totally given up on the quest for sobriety just a couple of months in. There were a couple good watering holes on the

NO WALK IN THE PARK

way home, and a liquor store nearby. I worked hard to stay out of trouble by not getting stupid until I got home.

Hey, if I was hurting anyone, it was just myself, right? Or so I thought.

Chapter 16

I spent more than two years in Greeley. I continued to hone my reporting skills, and learned that if I could be concise enough, my stories didn't get cut as often.

I learned another valuable lesson from the *Tribune's* star reporter and columnist, Mike Peters. I, like most reporters, secretly wanted my own column, and I occasionally talked about it with him. His edict was to always have a great *lede* (the first paragraph) to pull readers in, and a great conclusion to leave them wanting more.

Thanks to that advice, I would later get a 30+ year run and several awards with my personal column "A Pinch Of Salt." More about the *Grunion Gazette* column later, but its title was a play on my name I had tried to use in South Fork. Too hokey, Steve said.

I learned other journalism lessons at the *Trib*, including how to phone in a story. When it was close to deadline or I was at a remote location, I would literally call the office and read my story to someone else to type into the computer system.

You had to include punctuation and the rest – you might have seen it if you watched an old, old movie about newspaper reporters. "Period. Paragraph." I'll admit, I thought that was pretty cool.

I made plenty of acquaintances through work, primarily as sources for stories. I wasn't much for making friends though, with the newspaper staff or otherwise.

That might have been because I declined invitations for weekend activities; I had an obligation to go south to Pueblo. Still, I've always been a bit of a loner, and that continued.

And it was so much easier to drink that way. I didn't really understand the concept behind social drinking. The point of drinking was to get drunk, not to make friends.

I would stop at a bar occasionally, usually just to hear noise or watch a game. I'd sit alone.

Do you know what Rocky Mountain Oysters are? I discovered them at a little sports bar outside Greeley. They are fried bull genitals – sounds disgusting, but it was a pretty good treat. The supply was plentiful – that's how bulls become steers, you know. And they taste great with a shot and a beer.

Let's not talk about how I made it home on the motorcycle. But I always did.

Towards the end of 1986, a former *Tribune* reporter who had been hired away by the *Pueblo Chieftain* gave me a call. The *Chieftain* had an opening for a general assignment reporter – that's pretty high up the reporter food chain – and he wanted to put my name in. He knew I had a connection or two in town.

I had an obligation to give it a shot, didn't I? After all, I hadn't exactly been working hard on the marriage with wife two.

I still didn't have any kind of relationship with God, but I did believe I was a moral person. So I did the right thing, and took the interview.

On Dec. 1, 1986, I became a reporter for the *Pueblo Chieftain*. Oh, and moved in full time with wife two.

Chapter 17

I tried to slide back into the city where I had graduated from high school. I touched base with a few of my old classmates, and even joined a slow-pitch softball team with some of my high school baseball teammates.

It didn't really feel right, though, and the connections didn't stick. When we went out, it was with wife two's social circle. And I took longer and longer to get home from work.

I'll admit to not trying too hard to develop relationships at work either. The *Chieftain* was an old-school, family-owned paper in an old building. They were on the mainframe system, but the departments were separated by walls.

Even the city editor was behind a wall, with his own office. Not exactly conducive to camaraderie or collaboration.

There were ashtrays at each desk, though, and most of the time there was plenty of smoke in the air. I contributed my share.

I was getting paid hourly for the first time, and the paper's staff was unionized – a newspaper union is called a guild. I got myself in trouble with them pretty quickly.

I had been newspaper-raised to work until a story or project was done. I continued that practice in Pueblo and just put eight hours down on the timecard. At least I did until the union rep figured it out and told me I had to either quit after eight hours or put down overtime – I was making everybody else look bad.

So the next time I had a big story, I turned in some overtime. Management was not pleased, to say the least. Overtime had to be approved in advance.

I wasn't happy in this no-win situation. I never really resolved the issue.

Home wasn't exactly a bed of roses, either.

Wife two's number one goal once I was living there full time was to have a kid. That sounds like lots of romance and love-making, right?

Wrong. We were on a schedule, and we "did it" when it was time. After a couple of months without success, I found myself in a doctor's office, checking the sperm count. It had to be my fault, of course. I had fathered one child, but that wasn't necessarily proof of my sperm's ability, I guess.

Does alcohol kill sperm? I didn't look it up then, but it does, according to researchers today. It lowers sperm count and can even alter sperm characteristics.

But I don't think knowing that would have made any difference. I had no real desire to have another child.

I'm sure wife two wasn't happy either. There was no depth to the relationship, and very little happiness, let alone joy. Again, I'm sure it didn't help that I was working hard at finding ways to drink as much as possible without totally running off the rails.

God? I wasn't even thinking about Him. But He had something in store for me.

I had kept in touch with the gang at the *Tribune*, so I heard pretty quickly that they were looking for an assistant news editor. That's the person who writes headlines and decides what is going to go in the paper when the news editor isn't around.

I talked to the *Chieftain*'s top editor, just to see what he'd say. He opined that I wasn't cut out to be an editor – I was meant to be a reporter because I was good at that.

I'll bet you can guess how that impacted my decision.

I bargained my way into a weekly column in addition to the editing stuff. And they'd pay me more than the *Chieftain* was paying.

But it wouldn't have really mattered. I was going back to Greeley.

Chapter 18

The late 1980s and 1990s were a good time to own newspapers. There were a few chains, but for the most part, individuals and families had control.

At that time, the Rawlings family owned the *Chieftain*, along with its office and printing press. In Greeley, the *Tribune* was one of the flagship newspapers of a small outfit called Swift Communications.

A decently read newspaper was a profitable endeavor, especially in smaller markets. Neither city had its own television station. There were a couple local radio stations, but for the most part, any local business interested in advertising to bring in local customers had to go to the newspapers.

That included the preprints stuffed into the Sunday editions, and the classified ads that were the primary platforms to find a job, rent an apartment, sell a car, etc.

Because of the local or semi-local ownership, there was an honest commitment to the public. Reporting the news was a civic duty. It was up to the newspaper to be the government watchdog. Just as important was coverage of the local schools, including prep sports. Children are our future, you know.

Sure, the owners expected a profit. But that was only a part of why they were in business. They were considered a public service, and appreciated the identification.

Today, the *Pueblo Chieftain* is owned by the behemoth called Gannett Newspapers. They don't have a printing press – they don't even have an office building journalists can call home. The paper is printed in Denver and shipped to Pueblo.

The *Greeley Tribune* is part of an even larger conglomerate called Digital First, owned by the hedge fund called Alden Global Capital. There are some intermediaries – Prairie Mountain Media, which is a subsidiary of Media News, which is a subsidiary of Digital First.

Their building was sold in 2019, although they do still have a physical office in the city. The print paper only comes out four days a week and is printed at a regional printing plant.

Most of these giant media companies are on the stock exchange now, and the sole goal is profit. Decisions are made at corporate headquarters hundreds or thousands of miles away.

It's impossible to have a feeling of community spirit when you don't even know where the community is located.

I'll go into more detail about the causes of this demise in later chapters, but I had to get that off my chest – the *Greeley Tribune* and *Pueblo Chieftain* of today are barely ghosts of the papers I worked for back then. And that's a shame.

Chapter 19

Being a news desk editor is a totally different ball game than being a reporter. The focus on the desk is the finished product – what the paper looks like when the reader gets it.

It's a definite craft, just like reporting and writing, and I learned a lot. Did you know there used to be contests just for headline writing? It's a real skill, and the best at it are true artists.

In some ways, it was like being back in Creede, physically putting the paper together. I wasn't doing the physical labor, but I was checking the pages before they were sent to the plate room – it was my fault if a mistake made it into print, after all.

We were still on the mainframe computer system, and editorial stories came out separately from ads and pictures. Advertising was the key to profitability, and there were nearly as many people working in the advertising department as there were in editorial – more if you included the production department.

There was enough variety to keep me interested, and I did get to keep my hand in writing with a column once a week. I got put in charge of special projects, including an annual magazine that ran more than 100 pages.

I'll have to admit, though, that I missed chasing stories and writing every day. That guy in Pueblo might have had a point.

In the new Tribune building, it was one huge open space work area, with the only offices for the publisher and executive editor. The press was in its own large room. There was sort of a forced camaraderie – everyone got to know everyone else. That proved to be a factor later in my life.

I did get to experience one of those movie-moment thrills toward the end of my tenure there. It happened at the beginning of the U.S. participation in the Persian Gulf War on Jan. 17, 1991. The start of Operation Desert Storm came across the wire just after we had started that day's press run, and I got to run to the press room and yell "Stop The Presses!"

That was an adrenaline rush, to be sure.

The personal side of my life wasn't operating with the same sense of order. Wife two and I made it through one more Christmas, but I think we both knew it wasn't going anywhere.

I had made a friend of one of the Greeley city council members who happened to be an attorney, and with his help I drew up the divorce papers. We split up the debts — that means I took over most of them — and her only demand was to return to her maiden name. It was done quickly, and that was one less obligation I had to worry about.

Of course I had returned to daily drinking by that time. My apartment this time around was part of a four-plex, and I had one of the "garden" units. That meant it was half underground, and when you looked out the window it was at lawn level.

I called it the cave, and I took refuge there with a little television and a little bottle of booze. Lots of little bottles of booze.

Chapter 20

Alex's mom had turned to the ministry as her vocation – I thought she was crazy. Her father had been a minister, and after her 1980s fling she found the same vocation.

I still had little use for religion, and her brand of Methodist ministry was a pretty radical left-leaning approach. She was a woman pastor, after all. And I was still anti-religion.

But somehow, she was making that work in a small town on the Colorado plains. My opinion didn't matter, and I was still able to see my son fairly regularly. He was big enough by then that I was able to start teaching him how to play baseball, and that in turn prompted me to start umpiring for the Greeley Little League, both for some extra cash and for something to do.

Both of those life additions were due to the regular and limited schedule of my position at the paper. I was on a salary and could work more when I wanted, but I also was done when the paper was done, and I got regular days off.

So I started expanding my horizons, so to speak. There was a dog track about 20 miles away, and I had grown up with a grandfather racing greyhounds, so an occasional trip to the track was a treat. Of course I had a few drinks before firing up the motorcycle, and drinks were cheap at the track, so some of my bets didn't make much sense.

But it killed a night, and somehow the motorcycle ride didn't kill me.

Then there was the bar east of town famous for those Rocky Mountain Oysters. I discovered that I was a pretty good pool player after two or three drinks, so that was a pastime too. Unfortunately, both my pool playing and my behavior went downhill quickly after

NO WALK IN THE PARK

four or five drinks.

Eventually it was made clear I was no longer welcome there.

After the divorce from wife two, I avoided seeking female companionship for a while. I was pretty sure I wasn't worthy of anyone's affection – an opinion reinforced when I was drinking.

I was still functional, though, and did pretty decent work. I remained convinced that no one knew I was drinking hard, primarily by drinking alone and going to out-of-the-way bars when I did go out.

I even pulled off a road trip to Disneyland with Alex. I wouldn't drink until we stopped for the night, if at all. That was okay, except for the night we spent in Vegas.

I'm embarrassed, no, mortified, to say that I left him alone in the motel room "for a minute." I got back two hours later after a stint in the nearby casino.

Once again, God intervened, even though I didn't ask, and didn't acknowledge the blessing. Alex was sound asleep when I got back.

That trip became a column topic, with a semi-whine, semi-prideful essay about being a "Disneyland Dad." Apparently it struck a chord with a few folks, including a woman who sent me a message that we had a lot in common and we should talk.

I managed to turn the talk into a dinner date. She had three kids living with their father on the Colorado plains. I didn't ask for details; we hit it off and I discovered being around a woman again was a nice thing.

We ended up at my place – she didn't want to go back to her place. My desire fought right through the evening's consumption of alcohol, and it was a pretty amazing night.

Then she told me she was living with somebody else.

Chapter 21

I don't remember the timing of this life-changing event – I think I was into my second year of my second stint at the *Tribune*. It was undoubtedly a strange situation, but I thought I was in love. I knew I was in lust.

She convinced me she was unhappy with this other guy, not the least because there was little to no physical attraction. But she felt like she couldn't afford to move out, and I felt like there couldn't be a real relationship with her living with him.

So I started chasing after a few other women. But I kept coming back to her – the lady who had a lot in common with me. And there definitely was a physical attraction. I called her the compatible one – at least to myself.

I kept enough distance that my first love, alcohol, didn't intrude too much. She was a social drinker, and when we were out together, I apparently managed to keep it together.

Things eventually advanced enough that she found a way to move out on her own. She got a pretty good deal on a house and, with the help of renting out the basement to a friend, her dental assistant salary managed to barely stretch.

There was no suggestion that she move in with me. I don't think I offered – I had to keep my drinking to myself.

We did evolve into a relationship, though. And it quickly got more than a little rocky.

Yes, it was about alcohol, at least primarily. I couldn't help but get a little sloppy around her occasionally, and there was a time or two when I didn't show because I was "under the weather."

But it was more about me lying about my drinking, I think. Of course, I was lying to myself too, but she called me on it.

I kept stumbling along, alternating between feeling sorry for myself and being mad at her. I actually started drinking more.

Things came to a head one day when I went to lunch at a spot near work that served alcohol. I decided I needed a Scotch or two to calm the shakes from the previous night. I hadn't done that before.

But when I got back to work, my boss called me on it. We sat about two feet apart, so it was undoubtedly easy to get a whiff.

He was kind – he took me off campus and told me if it happened again, he'd have to report me, and probably fire me. That was enough to scare me.

I talked it over with the compatible one, and she essentially told me the same thing – quit or I'm going to fire you.

I knew I had to do something, but I really didn't want to go back to AA. I was afraid someone would know me, I remembered the tough times I had had before in AA, especially with that Higher Power thing… I had lots of excuses.

So I decided to quit on my own.

That sounds like a foolish decision, and it likely was. But believe it or not, I did it.

I stopped cold turkey, as the expression goes. I suffered through withdrawals, and I started smoking more. But my mind cleared.

And I was even able to take the compatible one out and watch her have a drink or two. A new thing, non-alcoholic beer, was just coming out back then, so I compromised with that.

It wasn't perfect, but it was close.

Chapter 22

Journalism, and newspapering in particular, was still a viable option at the end of the '80s and beginning of the '90s. I was settled in and had learned a lot about the graphic and layout side of creating newspapers. The business model and the technology hadn't changed significantly.

I also noticed a blonde working in the graphics department. We struck up a friendship, but that was it. The compatible one and I were pretty hot and heavy. We'll revisit the blonde later.

There's one thing about working at a small- to medium-sized paper in a small- to medium-sized town, at least if you're in management. You tend to settle in.

Early-career reporter types back in the day seldom stayed in one spot more than four years. It's just a matter of working your way up the career ladder. (Notice that I had followed that timeline, too.)

I was right at four years in my second stint at the *Tribune*, and I had to admit, I was missing the adrenaline rush of chasing stories. What I was doing wasn't boring, but it wasn't exciting either.

And everyone above me in the editor chain – the news editor, the city editor, the editorial page editor, the executive editor – all had families and an established life in Greeley. It was clear I wasn't going up that particular ladder.

The compatible one and I were getting along exceptionally well. We began talking about the future. I had been sober for six or eight months, so it seemed like it might stick.

So I took the plunge and asked her to marry me. We were both a little gunshy (she had gone through the marry-divorce bit too), but I really did want to take the next step.

She ultimately agreed, but with one condition. She wanted to live by the ocean. All this time in Colorado, she was a closet California girl.

So I started looking for jobs on the West Coast. It wasn't as easy as it is today with JournalismJobs.com, but there was a network of newspaper associations where you could find what was out there.

We were so certain that it would all fall into place that I gave up my apartment and moved into her house. I didn't give notice at the *Tribune* though – I'd learned that lesson back in South Fork.

It took some time, and I sent out several resumes. Again, the waiting was hard, and I'll admit to thinking a drink or two would make it easier. But I left it alone.

I finally got a response from the *Oxnard Press-Courier*. Oxnard is on the coast just south of Ventura, and about 60 miles north of Los Angeles. It sounded pretty perfect.

A couple of phone interviews fleshed out the offer. I'd start as the night editor and move up when the news editor retired, which was supposed to be soon.

I expected an invitation to come see the operation and Oxnard before the offer was final. Instead, I got a call saying the job was mine if I wanted it. When could I start?

Here's perhaps the only bit of advice I'll offer in this entire book – never take a job over the phone.

We had less than a month to figure out how to get married, get packed and move to California. We did it sort of in reverse. The U-Haul was packed and the car on the trailer the day we were married. Our honeymoon was a one-way trip to Oxnard, California.

Chapter 23

We pulled into Oxnard on Sept. 30, 1991. I remember the date because it was my birthday and we went to Denny's to eat because I could get a free meal.

It was a different world back then. We started apartment hunting the next day, and by evening we had a place rented. I checked in with the paper and got my start date, then spent the next couple of days trying to familiarize myself with the city.

The compatible one started looking for a job. My pay was higher than at the *Tribune*, but it cost more to live in California even back then. We needed two paychecks.

She had had a great working relationship with the dentist in Greeley – they were close friends. She had a strong resume, and found a job in the first couple of weeks.

But this dentist would not be a good friend.

We had my car and my motorcycle for transportation, so I rode the bike to work and she took the car. I had the swing shift – afternoon until the paper was finished – while she started early in the morning and worked until 4 or so.

In other words, once we both started working, we didn't see much of each other during the week. But I'd say we were pretty happy newlyweds.

We weren't happy employees, though.

There's really no other way to describe the *Oxnard Press-Courier* – this was a bad paper. It was in an old building in downtown Oxnard, with the newsroom separated from the presses by a thin wall. The place seemed dark during the day, and worse when the sun went down – when I worked.

The quality of the editorial content was pretty poor too. As a whole, the paper (and to some extent the city) was the poor cousin to the upscale city of Ventura and the *Ventura County Star* just up the coast. And the *Press-Courier* bunch didn't seem to be putting up much of a fight.

I was relegated to doing stuff like putting the weekend advertorial auto section together. It was, to put it in today's parlance, tough to engage.

The compatible one was having an even harder time. This dentist was a harsh taskmaster, and verbally abusive. The compatible one was naturally friendly and upbeat, but this guy was grinding her down. And I usually had to go to work before she was done telling me her woes from the day.

We made it through Christmas, and managed to have a few good times together in the surrounding environs. But we were living for the weekends, and had started to talk about how this might not have been such a good decision after all.

God was moving in His mysterious ways, and taking His time while He was at it. But I didn't consider taking it up with Him. I was doing my own thing.

I had made acquaintances with the second shift crew, and eventually got invited to come by their favorite bar for an after-work beer. I said no a couple of times, without explaining why. Then I broke down and stopped by to talk and have a non-alcoholic beer.

That worked – until somebody put a real beer in front of me. Funny how it tasted just like a non-alcoholic beer.

Anyone in Alcoholics Anonymous will tell you that the first drink inevitably leads you down the slippery slope. That's why they call it a slip when an alcoholic goes back to drinking.

But I'll tell you that I handled that first beer just fine. And when a couple weeks later I had a couple of beers, I handled that just fine too.

I handled it except for the guilt I felt. And the fear that the compatible one would find out. That's why I made it through the Oxnard days without a real problem.

Chapter 24

I was working on what was supposed to be a book mainly because I didn't have any other writing outlet. (I might still have that half-assed effort in a drawer somewhere.) But when it became clear I wasn't going to be on the *New York Times'* bestseller list any time soon, the compatible one and I agreed it was time to get serious about an escape plan.

God gently put a Sunday *Los Angeles Times* in my hand the very next weekend. I didn't know it then, but that newspaper was God shaping the rest of my life.

Remember, this was still the time of printed help wanted ads. Sunday newspapers, especially the *Los Angeles Times*, were well-known for thick classified ad sections. Business owners and property owners knew that's where people would be looking for jobs, places to live and more.

So I splurged and paid my $1.50 for the pound of newsprint that was the Sunday *Times*.

And after shaking my head at all the manual labor opportunities I had, I came across an ad for an executive editor at a weekly newspaper called the *Grunion Gazette* down in Long Beach.

It had everything I was looking for – it was an all-local community newspaper. It was privately owned. It was looking to fill the position as soon as possible.

I'll admit to my hands shaking a bit as I showed the ad to the compatible one. We knew nothing about Long Beach. I looked it up on a map – 20 miles south of Los Angeles and on the coast. There was a big port there.

Good enough for us.

I retooled my resume to emphasize the do-it-all aspects of the job in South Fork and Creede. I cranked up the sincerity in the cover letter, pushing the writing and photography skills and experience without mentioning that they might be a bit rusty.

The compatible one proofread and approved. We took the package to the post office to make sure it got mailed.

A week later, I got a call. We set up an interview and a few days later I headed down the highway to Long Beach, some 90 miles down the coast from Oxnard.

I found out at the interview that the Sunday I saw the ad was the only time the owners put it in the *Los Angeles Times*. God moves in mysterious ways, but He definitely moves!

The interview went well. John and Fran Blowitz had had successful early careers in L.A., and John had wanted to get back to his college journalism roots after flying pretty high with television and movie marketing. They had purchased a little tabletop neighborhood paper named the *Grunion Gazette* in one of Long Beach's upscale neighborhoods, and had already built it up to a going enterprise.

We had the same philosophy when it came to community papers — write about what the community wanted to know about. That meant their kids, their neighbors, their businesses and themselves.

Then you could add some of the stuff they needed to know, like what the city was doing with their money and how their part of town was changing. John and Fran's focus on advertising was all local — business owners talking to the local customers.

They were both hard workers, and liked to do things themselves. John ran the editorial side and Fran handled the advertising, each with a small staff. I won't say we fit like a glove, but we fit pretty well.

I and the compatible one were back in Long Beach the next week apartment hunting.

When I gave my notice at the Oxnard paper, there was an undercurrent of jealousy in the newsroom. And once again, God was looking out for me even though I didn't know or acknowledge it. The *Press-Courier* shut down less than a year later, in early 1993.

Things got better for the compatible one and me almost immediately after we moved to Long Beach. The previous editor at the paper actually hung around for a month to train me on the fancy new Apple equipment and introduce me around town (John liked to do that too). The compatible one had been soured on the dentistry industry with her last experience, but latched onto a clerical job pretty quickly.

That Apple equipment was the leading edge of the next generation in newspaper technology. There were Macintosh Plus desktop computers, all connected by Ethernet hardwiring, and a second-generation Laser printer that could actually print an 11"x14" tabloid page. (We more often printed the regular 8 ½"x11" page top and bottom, and spliced them together.)

Software had advanced rapidly too. There were now graphics programs that allowed you to manipulate text and create pages on the computer. That graphics program seemed like something out of science fiction.

There was still plenty of physical putting things together, and advertising and pictures had to be added onto the final printouts, but it was a quantum leap forward for me.

And I was back to where I had control over the whole editorial process, from interviewing sources and writing stories to creating headlines and approving pages. I was in my element.

Chapter 25

My timing was both really good and really bad when it came to taking this new job.

I started on March 1, 1992. The 1992 Toyota Grand Prix of Long Beach was on April 12. That meant I had just enough time to get my press credentials and photo pass so I could cover the largest street race in the country, and the second largest open-wheel car race after the Indianapolis 500.

Long Beach's Grand Prix is actually three days worth of hot times at the track with undercard races, including the infamous Toyota Pro/Celebrity Race (it ended in 2016) where I could get up close and personal with celebrities and celebrity wannabes. I hate to admit it, but at least that first year I knew more about those celebrities than I knew about the IndyCar drivers who were the real stars of the show.

But I was able to sniff out the spots on the circuit where a press pass could get you in for a free drink, even if it might be just cheap champagne. It was one big party, and I got to watch it.

I may have already said this, but I'll say it again – the very best thing about my newspaper career is the incredible number of things I got to do and experience. The Grand Prix has consistently been one of the best.

Then just two weeks later, April 29, to be exact, Los Angeles and the surrounding area exploded. The 1992 Riots were sparked by the innocent verdict for four Los Angeles city police officers after they were seen beating Rodney King (whose later plea of "Can't we all just get along?" became iconic) in view of a video camera. It was hard to call the verdict anything but a farce.

The rioting reached the 20 miles south to Long Beach on the second day. There were barricades in the streets. The Long Beach

CHAPTER 25

Department of Motor Vehicles office was burned to the ground and many stores looted.

This was also the very first week I was in charge of the papers on my own. The ambulance chaser in me kicked in, and even though I didn't know where I was going most of the time, I went out to take pictures. I only got chased by a looter once. He didn't catch me, but he did drop his case of beer.

I got the paper out, the riots ended and the recriminations began. I made one misstep – my lead headline called them "race riots," which they were, but Long Beach's African American community objected. It took me a while to regain their trust, but it also gave me a leg up on establishing a reputation as someone who told it like it was.

It didn't take long for me to get back to working 60 hours a week. A chunk of that came on Tuesday nights, which was the editorial deadline for that week's *Grunion*. In addition to completing my own writing and editing copy from the stringers, I put the pages together for the final pasteup the next day.

I bragged about the technological advances earlier, but this still was the early days of computer-based work. Those printers were slooow. It took 15 minutes or more to print one page, and the snazzy graphic computer program always had to think a bit before following through on a command.

Those first few weeks, I didn't get done before 2 a.m. It would be a year before I was able to lock the door before midnight.

The compatible one took most of this in stride. She had made some friends at work, and part of my job was to go to occasional social events, which we attended together. I didn't drink when she was with me.

But I was drinking again. I had convinced myself that peppermint schnapps smelled like breath mints, and those little one-shot airline bottles were cheap. I didn't care much for vodka, but tried it too because someone told me once that you couldn't smell it on your breath.

◄ NO WALK IN THE PARK

And my main goal on Tuesday nights, once I had the routine down, was to get done in time to make it to the bar before last call. I got my favorite then – Scotch on the rocks. You'd say it Scotch rocks to get the bartender pouring just a touch sooner. The compatible one was sound asleep by the time I got home around 2 a.m.

As usual, I was sure I was getting away with it all, and everything was fine. Life had its ups and downs – the compatible one had to change jobs a year or so in – but essentially we were learning to love Long Beach.

Until one night when we decided to go to dinner with a couple of her friends, then take them to the downtown blues club.

Chapter 26

We'd been in Long Beach for a few years by then – 1994, I believe. The papers – in addition to the *Grunion* we published a Monday edition called the *Downtown Gazette* – were doing well. John and Fran believed in investing in the company, including staff, and I had one full-time reporter and another part-time reporter, soon to be two.

I was being invited to quite a few social events in my capacity as the *Grunion* editor, and the compatible one often accompanied me. She gradually got used to seeing me with a glass of wine, but I was careful not to over-indulge when she was around.

A couple the compatible one had connected with at work suggested a double date one weekend. We could have dinner together downtown, then perhaps go listen to some music. There was a blues club in town that booked some good acts.

At dinner, I discovered that the other couple were wine connoisseurs – at least they talked a good game. So we had a couple of bottles with dinner. Maybe three.

Then we headed on over to the blues club. This wasn't exactly a place with a long wine list, so it was time to switch to mixed drinks. Unfortunately, I decided I should be able to have a drink too.

We had a good time, I think. I danced with the compatible one's good friend more than a bit. If I remember correctly, the compatible one didn't seem interested in dancing with me.

I should have taken the clue.

This was on a Saturday night. Our regular routine on Sunday morning was to sleep late, and get up to watch *CBS Sunday Morning* while I read the paper. No church services; we were not believers and looked down on those who were.

I knew I'd messed up the night before, but I was still a bit shook up with the silent treatment I received. I finally tried to force a conversation.

"You lied," was about all I got for the first few minutes. She was talking about me swearing up and down I'd only have a glass of wine once in a while.

I broke down and confessed about how I was regularly sneaking around and drinking again – past experience had taught me how to do that. Only it didn't work quite as well as it had in the past.

"You lied."

That lying thing is something else past experience had taught me. Any self-respecting alcoholic has learned that lesson well. For the most part, our lives while drinking – at least if you are still trying to function in life – is one big lie.

But this time the contrite confession didn't work. The compatible one made it clear that I wasn't compatible with her if I was drinking and lying about it. I'm pretty sure the lying part was the bigger issue.

So I offered to move out "for a month or two" until I could get my act back together. Naturally I thought she'd say that wasn't necessary. We could work it out, right?

Wrong.

She opined that a separation would be a good idea. We had done this (just not seeing each other) once before in Greeley and it had worked to get me on the straight and narrow then.

I happened to know that one of my coworkers had a converted garage for rent, so I followed through.

I was out in a week. I was left to my own devices again.

That wasn't a good thing.

Chapter 27

I have to stress that I managed to continue doing good work at the newspaper. Oh, I was not necessarily a joy to be around, but we were putting out a paper that continued to gain respect.

John continued to invest in equipment, and our graphics got better and faster. We had begun putting together a special edition every year for the annual Grand Prix, that huge road race that impressed me so much when I first got to town.

We cut a deal to hand the paper out near the race entrances. It was free, had the race schedule and lots of people grabbed one. It was a kick to walk around the course and see my work in so many hands.

I believe that was the first place we ran a color picture in print. John was kind of perversely proud that he was one of the last publishers to move from black-and-white-only photography. And color was more than a bit of a pain, what with separations for each color and the registration issues at the printing plant.

But technology advances were picking up speed, and we entered the "modern era" pretty quickly. It allowed us to grow. There were several display ad sales people, two classified advertising representatives, a three-person production team and I had two full-time reporters along with a part-timer and a stable of stringers.

We hit a pinnacle when our Grand Prix edition totalled 104 pages, with another 60 pages of regular newspaper sections. That included 10 or 11 pages of classified ads – the *Grunion* was the must-read publication if you were looking for a place to live either as a renter or an owner – and two pages of Personal Ads.

Those personal ads were free. The money was made on the 1-900 toll phone calls people made to connect with the people advertising. It was the hook-up approach of preference before on-line dating.

This was Fran's baby. She came up with an even better idea (at least to my mind) to play off the Personals with a *Grunion Gazette* Valentine's Date Night. It was a dance party where people would submit an application and we would make matches for the evening. They had done one before I got there, and it made a little money for charity.

Like everything else *Grunion* at the time, Date Night grew. We connected with the heart programs at Long Beach's three major hospitals, donating money and accepting the volunteer help they had to offer.

We moved the event to the Queen Mary, and soon had more than a thousand attendees. You could literally feel the hormones flowing when you walked through the room. And we'd raise $30,000, $40,000 and once nearly $50,000 in a single night.

I got to act like a big shot at the events, running around collecting money and such. It was still mostly cash in those days, so that was fun. I got to spend a few nights on the ship, and the bartenders treated me right.

One year, when I was single again (I'll get back to that in a minute), I "sold" a date with me. That same year, there was a bungee tower next to the Queen, and I collected donations for people to see me bungee jump in a tuxedo. I pulled off both the jump and the date without falling on my face.

Good times.

But there was this thing called the Internet on the horizon, creating a cloud. We didn't realize at the time just how big a cloud it would be.

Chapter 28

Back to the cave version 3 – the converted garage. After a week of self-pity drinking, I determined I was going to do something about my plight.

I found an AA meeting within walking distance, and started attending. It was an AA-dedicated space, and a group of hardcore members ran the show. That worked for a bit.

Unfortunately for me, I also rediscovered the joys of drinking alone. The liquor store was closer than the AA meeting room, and I took advantage. I wasn't responsible to the compatible one anymore, so as long as I could make it to work, it was all good, right?

A month away from the compatible one turned into a few months, then more than a half year. It was clear – to me at least – that I wasn't ever going to be good enough for her to accept me back. I'm good at telling myself how bad I am.

We didn't own anything of significance and California makes it nearly as easy to get a divorce as Nevada does. I gathered the paperwork for a do-it-yourself divorce, and we agreed to sign the dotted line.

It was, and is, sad. I don't think it is an exaggeration to say that it was the lowest point in my life to date. I was 41 years old, divorced for the third time, living in a converted garage, a sometimes-drunk with nothing much to show for a 15-year career in journalism.

I won't presume to judge the compatible one's state of mind, but I believe it was a sad day for her too.

I could have turned to God at that time, but I didn't. Instead, I relied on myself, getting buried in work during the day and a bottle at night.

NO WALK IN THE PARK

There was plenty of work.

It was 1995, and a dark time for Long Beach, too. The city had been a Navy town since before World War II, with the Long Beach Naval Station and Navy Shipyard providing jobs and money.

But as the 1990s began (and I showed up in Long Beach), the nation decided it was time to cash in the "peace dividend." That required base closures to reduce military costs, and Long Beach's Naval Station was one of the casualties – the process was completed in 1994.

We still had the shipyard, which was responsible for $757 million in 1990 dollars annually in the region. But San Diego, where old admirals went to die, wanted all of the Navy, including the shipyard.

A couple of powerful Republican Congressmen from S.D. started twisting arms, and on June 23, 1995, the Base Closure and Realignment Commission voted to shut the Long Beach shipyard down.

I had developed strong connections at City Hall, including with Mayor Beverly O'Neill and City Manager Jim Hankla. That allowed me to closely follow the efforts the city government would make to rebuild Long Beach and leave the Naval legacy behind.

Putting my ability to explain complex situations in understandable terms to work, I became the go-to when the city wanted to tell residents what they were trying to do. By making sure to explain the potential downsides too, I served those residents with stories that built the *Grunion*'s credibility.

There was less public trust in the media in the 1990s than in previous decades, but we still were the primary information source, particularly when it came to government activity. There still was a truth to be told, and we were the place to find it.

Yes, I am well aware of the irony that I was considered a source for truth while I was living the lie of an alcoholic's life. It was getting harder and harder to fool even myself that I was getting by.

I think it was about then, maybe it was the following year, that

CHAPTER 28

Fran "suggested" I see one of her friends who happened to be a psychologist about my "depression." I was a reluctant subject when it came to counseling, but it did seem to make a bit of difference. The prescribed antidepressants lifted the cloud a little, but didn't do more than slow the alcohol consumption.

I was getting by, with a little help from my friends.

Chapter 29

I won't lie — the late 1990s are a bit of a blur in my memory. The papers were doing well, and technology improved year over year, making it a bit easier to get production done.

Email came into its own, at least for the editor side of me. Contributors were able to send me files that I could download, edit and get into the system. Worst case scenario, I could copy the text from an email and put it into a word document. Tons better and faster than retyping things.

Trying to convince readers to do that instead of mailing in hand-written letters was a constant battle, especially given our reader demographic (well-off, which means older). But I truly enjoyed the fact that at least some of the community seemed engaged in the discussion of the community we promoted.

Continuing down the communication path, I remember being excited when John and Fran gave me a Nokia cell phone. The excitement remained until I realized it meant that they could reach me whenever they wanted.

That was sort of okay. I was dealing with my single life by burying myself in work, with sporadic escapes into a bottle. If I was working on something, I wasn't thinking about what a failure I was as a person.

And people recognized me on the street — my picture was in the paper every week along with my column. The ego got stroked fairly regularly.

I was still drinking fairly regularly too. But the confidence started rebuilding, especially after a former employee turned real estate agent convinced me I could buy a condo for pretty much the same price I was paying for rent.

CHAPTER 29

Getting out of the cave improved my outlook on life, and I actually started looking at women again when I went to events. As the *Grunion* editor, I was expected to go to a lot of events.

Despite my loner tendencies, I became involved in community organizations, in the beginning largely at John's urging. He believed, and I agreed, that calling yourself a community paper meant that you had to be in the community.

This was God setting me up for a lifetime of service, but I wasn't aware of that at the time. I was just following orders and polishing my image.

This push to get involved had a side effect that ultimately colored my career and status in Long Beach. I was being asked to participate in city government-sponsored studies and panels. The mayor, Beverly O'Neill, asked me to serve on a task force to study ways to "end" homelessness. Then I was asked to be on the task force to create the city's next strategic plan.

If you are a journalist, and likely even if you aren't, you know that I was skirting concepts of conflict of interest here. It's difficult to argue that you are being objective when you write about city government if you are involved in that government.

My argument was that I didn't write news stories about anything I was directly involved in – I had staff who could do that. I'll admit now that I probably crossed the line when I wrote my column about those topics, though, and I did that fairly often.

But from the very beginning, I had been writing columns and editorials about news and issues I had written stories about as well – occasionally even in the same edition. It was the reality of a small-staffed community newspaper that we weren't able to draw a bright line between the opinion page and the news pages like our larger brethren did. I explained the difference between the front page and the opinion page at least two or three times a year, but I'm not sure that explanation ever took with a lot of the readers.

What did take was my consistent demand for seeking all sides.

NO WALK IN THE PARK

I'm happy to say I built a reputation as someone who told a story in a balanced manner, keeping opinion out of the news. Doing that for 10, 20, 30 years built credibility with our readers.

This issue got even harder once I started serving on appointed city boards. Thank God I was sober by then and was able to both walk the tightrope and handle the blowback a bit better.

But that's down the road. Let me tell you about the woman I'll call the righteous one first.

Chapter 30

Long Beach was recovering nicely in the late 1990s under Mayor O'Neill and City Manager Hankla. The shift away from the Navy and toward a more tourist-oriented waterfront economy was gaining traction, and the city was able to look forward with some optimistic planning exercises.

I continued to keep up a pretty solid public face despite drinking myself to sleep most nights, and was asked to participate in some of that planning. One of those endeavors put me in the same discussion group with a city official I had seen from afar, but had never interacted with personally.

It was the righteous one. She was brilliant, upper management, and very pretty.

After engaging in discussions during a couple of meetings, it seemed appropriate to offer some small talk as we walked to our cars. Then, serendipitously, we were both at a social event — I saw her across a crowded room. And despite the free booze, I made it my goal to further our relationship beyond acquaintance.

We had many similar interests, primarily the well-being of the city of Long Beach. We knew many of the same people, and traveled in the same circles. We were of an age, and for some reason she was unattached at the time.

A date turned into a night of talking on her porch until well past the witching hour, and we were suddenly in a relationship.

By this time, I had plenty of experience in keeping my act together while still having a drink or three. It was easier when I was motivated, as in trying to ingratiate myself with a woman.

One method is the time-honored alcoholic trick of having a couple of drinks before the evening begins. In this situation, I often downed a couple of shots of peppermint schnapps on my way to her place, thereby "relaxing" enough so I didn't drink a lot while around her.

Things progressed to the level of sleepovers – always her place, not mine. Soon there was a bit of a weekend routine. A Saturday night date, followed by a Sunday trip to her church for services before parting ways to prepare for the next week.

You're right – I've been saying all along that I had no use for religion, and if anything thought that if there was a God, He was against me. I was certainly too bad a person to find any favor with Him.

But the church clearly was important to the righteous one, so I went along. There was no actual discussion about faith between us, so I was safe.

I suspect I'm not the only man who was ever lured to church by a woman.

I thought I was just playing along to keep the righteous one happy – we even double-dated with a married couple who were church friends of hers.

But I gradually found myself listening to the sermons, the songs, and the prayers. This wasn't the repressive Catholicism of my youth.

I started looking around and watching people's faces as they worshiped. And one day I heard my brain say, "I think I might want what these people have."

It was a small step, but it was a step – a glimmer, if you will. But there would be some nasty stuff before the glimmer could become a light.

Chapter 31

I've done a lot of stupid things in my life due to alcohol, and they didn't stop when I connected with the righteous one.

This phase of my addiction had progressed to the point where I needed to have a drink to keep from getting the shakes. I pretty consistently stopped on my way to the righteous one's condo to get a shot or two. The liquor store was only a half-mile or so from her place, so they were literally shots.

One incident stands out in my memory.

It was a Saturday, and I had taken my car to get an oil change. I thought I'd impress the righteous one with a night at a comedy club. Of course I checked with her first!

I made the reservation at the comedy club, but I was still third in line for the oil change. I spied a liquor store across the street. It was early afternoon, so…

I hadn't been to this particular store, and they didn't carry the airplane bottles I was so fond of. So I opted for a bottle of vodka – I think it was a half-pint, but it might have been a pint.

Done with the day's chores, I decided to go home and "rest" before the big date. The rest involved drinking the entire bottle and passing out.

When I came to, it was twilight. I was a combination of hung over and still inebriated. But I had something I said I was going to do, so off I went.

By the time I got to her place, I was literally ill – I might have stopped and vomited a time or two.

It had to be the flu, I told her. A 24-hour bug maybe? Or food poisoning was a possibility.

She took it in stride, fed me four Tylenol PM pills and put me to bed. It took four more an hour later before I fell into a fitful sleep.

The embarrassment was just as painful as the hangover the next morning. But I managed to accompany her to church before I took my leave.

One thing I still don't understand. The righteous one never brought up my drinking. There was no heartfelt discussion, no dire ultimatums. I suspect there were some sidelong glances of disgust, but no confrontation.

I know she had suffered some pretty traumatic experiences with a former partner, so maybe that's why. More likely, the actual relationship wasn't strong enough to fight for in her eyes.

We broke up in December. I had already purchased Christmas gifts, and she tried to give them back. I refused. It was a sad day.

But Alex, now 19 and a college student, was coming to visit for the holidays, so I had to get it together. And lo and behold, I actually stopped drinking. I was self-aware enough to think it would likely just be until Alex went back to Colorado, but I made it through the withdrawals, and we had a decent holiday.

I even set it up to go to the New Year's Eve party on the Queen Mary with Alex. It was a big bash, but I made it through the night without a drink.

When Alex went home, instead of heading to the liquor store I headed back to that AA hall. I thought I had really hit bottom.

Besides, there was another relationship in the wings.

Oh, and I went out to find another church. Turns out I wanted to pursue this religion thing, but didn't want the discomfort of seeing the righteous one there. It was hard enough to see her at city events.

A friend recommended a pretty conservative church – Grace Community Church of Seal Beach, in the town just south of Long Beach. It turns out that guy didn't attend that often, but I kind of liked it. I just sat and listened, but that was enough at the time.

Chapter 32

Do you remember the great Prince song "Party Like It's 1999?" Do you remember why 1999 was such a big deal, even beyond the fact that turning the century calendar is always a big deal?

It was all about computers. By 1999, our reliance on computers had become a real thing. They were much more than big calculators, or fancy processors.

By the late 1990s, computers had taken over things like airline schedules – heck, airplane controls, too. Our government relied on them for everything from payrolls to missile deterrence systems.

The Internet – a mysterious extension of computers – had established itself by 1996. In 1999, there were 150 million internet users worldwide, with more than half of that number in the United States. And the Internet meant online news outlets, both independent and affiliated with newspapers. We were slow to join the club, but started putting up static PDF (portable document format, for the non-nerds) copies of the print edition. By the end of the century, we had begun a "real" website with a webmaster and everything.

I'm pretty sure Prince wasn't thinking about the catastrophic consequences for newspapers from computers and the Internet when he wrote "Like It's 1999." But it was about an expected computer catastrophe.

The big worry was the fact that computers, as complicated as they had become, still operated on a basic 0 or 1 binary system of computation. And there were legitimate (or it sounded like it at the time) concerns that shifting the date from 1999 to 2000 would essentially cause the computer world to blow its collective mind and bring on the apocalypse.

As you know, that didn't happen. But it was a good excuse for another "end of the world" party. Hence, Party like it's 1999.

The big New Year's Eve bash downtown that had booked big acts in previous years had been canceled for lack of ticket sales – not everyone was following Prince's advice, clearly. There were significantly fewer partiers aboard the Queen, too. But that's where Alex and I went so I could take pictures.

Around 11 p.m., midnight Colorado time, I made a phone call. It was to a woman named Maria.

Maria was that blonde graphic artist in Greeley I had made friends with while working at the *Tribune*. We had become friends, and she had let me know that things weren't great at home. She had three kids and a husband who was less than pleasant or supportive.

She had reached out a time or two since I'd moved to California, including one long talk while I was still married to the compatible one where she said she was being verbally abused and it was getting worse. I had offered what comfort I could, and suggested it might be time to escape.

She eventually took my advice and moved out with her kids. She had a full-time job at a publication in Greeley, but I don't know how she made ends meet.

After the compatible one and I had separated over the drinking and lying, I took some solace in reconnecting with Maria. We began talking on the phone fairly frequently, and I arranged two or three visits over the next couple of years.

I had distanced myself from Maria during the time the righteous one and I were together, but never cut it off. We offered mutual support, and I didn't want to give that up.

I don't know what made me decide to call that night. Maybe I was more lonely than I realized, watching all the other couples partying. Maybe it was a God thing.

I didn't know it at the time, but that New Year's Eve was another

CHAPTER 32

turning point in my life set up by God. That phone call was the beginning of a new relationship.

When we hung up, the conversation ended with "I miss you" – from both of us. That meant a lot.

Chapter 33

It should come as no surprise that the first six months of 2000 were pretty momentous. Once the world got over the joy/disappointment that the end of the world hadn't come, there was lots of talk about new beginnings.

I liked that idea. A lot.

I became a regular attender at church, and a semi-regular attender at the AA group that met in one of the church's meeting rooms. In both settings, I was an observer, rarely a participant.

I had little slips here and there, but for the most part stayed sober. I buried myself in work, which has always been my primary coping mechanism when things are hard.

I also had started to get more involved in Long Beach issues and organizations. I had been on the Chamber of Commerce board for a couple of years at John's urging – I took his place when he termed out. Then I was asked to join the Public Corporation for the Arts board, a quasi-governmental group that served as the city's Arts Council.

In the beginning of 2000, I was asked to be president of the PCA board. It was an honor and certainly stroked my ego. I really did think I could make a difference, too. I loved theater and the arts and knew enough artists to know they were almost always terrible at business.

The *Grunion* was hanging in there, still producing large weekly papers and regularly beating the daily *Press-Telegram* in both news coverage and advertising. We still weren't making any money on the website – no one was, really – but I still had full time and part time staff, and the advertising department was strong in both display and classified advertising.

CHAPTER 33

But a little outfit called Craigslist had a coming-out party in 1999, acting as a free bulletin board for people selling stuff, renting apartments and more. By our first paper in 2000, our classified ad section had gone down to five pages after averaging eight or more in the past few years.

It was a sign of things to come.

Computers were improving by leaps and bounds, and the printing process was as well. We started using more color, at least on the front page, and our circulation for the *Grunion* and *Downtown* peaked at more than 60,000 papers a week.

Two-thirds of that circulation was free home delivery to selected high-end neighborhoods. East Long Beach had large neighborhoods of multi-million and million-dollar homes – one called Naples, complete with canals; Belmont Shore where land was so valuable no one had yards; historic Belmont Heights and Alamitos Heights; etc. *Grunions* were on every doorstep every Thursday morning.

Business districts weren't quite Rodeo Drive of Beverly Hills fame, but they were upscale. Our sales reps, both display and classified, were able to claim that *Gazette* readers read their papers from cover to cover, including the ads, because it was true.

I worked hard to be sure we had something for everyone, from hard news to a horoscope. We had become a bit less parochial; at least we were covering more citywide news and less Belmont Shore-only stuff. Still, our readers depended on us to find out what was happening in their neighborhoods, so we wrote about a lot of the "little things."

I learned way back in the South Fork days that people liked to read about people, and in particular about their children, or at least children they had a connection with. One of my mantras to my writers was to try to tell stories through people, and they excelled at doing just that.

I was still doing a lot of reporting and writing – remember that we were totally local content (except for that horoscope) and we had to fill a lot of pages. We were proud of the fact that we had an open (no ads) opinion page, just like the "big boys." John had a column each week, and I had one too. We had an occasional guest editorial and lots of letters to the editor – people like to read their own writing too.

That all-local thing was important to me. It was so important, in fact, that I frequently turned down potential stories or calendar items simply because they were on the wrong side of the city line. It made some folks mad, but it did set up some clear priorities.

There was a reason for that policy beyond my stubbornness. If we were going to survive as a community newspaper against the already burgeoning number of news and information sources on the Internet, we had to fill a specific niche. We had to be the only place where people could find the information they wanted and needed about their own neighborhood, their own city council district and their own city.

We were doing exactly that, and it worked.

Chapter 34

I was thankful that the phone company no longer charged for long-distance calls by the minute.

That long-distance Happy New Year from the Queen Mary launched what I can only call a rapidly escalating relationship between Maria and myself. We spent a lot of time in the evenings, usually late – after her kids were fed and in bed – on the phone or emailing back and forth.

It had the added benefit of occupying my thoughts so I could stay away from the booze. I still went to that Alcoholics Anonymous meeting once a week or so.

My duties as the PCA president and the newspaper guy kept me going to social events, and that was admittedly difficult – the good parties had open bars. I occasionally leaned on O'Doul's, the go-to non-alcoholic beer at the time. Tonic water with a twist in hand usually kept people from asking questions, too.

After the righteous one, it was kind of refreshing to see myself as a bit of a white knight when it came to Maria. She was in a tough spot, trying to raise three kids on her own after her divorce. I could bring a little light into her life with phone calls, and we even managed to meet up a time or two.

I got her out to Long Beach once with a promise to go to Disneyland. The one day we were able to go, it rained. Hard.

Did you know that rainy days are good days to go to Disneyland? At least they were in 2000, because there were no crowds. We got to ride pretty much everything, with time to burn. I had her back at my place and warming up under a blanket before the day was done.

I had begun to daydream about convincing her to move to

California. I could ride in on my white horse and rescue her from all the dragons at her door.

Of course I hadn't thought about the kids. The oldest, Aimee, was graduating from high school that year and had college plans, but there were still Charlotte and John, starting high school and in junior high, respectively. I think they were 14 and 11. A complication, to be sure.

I made it out to Colorado for high school graduation season so I could watch Alex get his diploma, and managed to spend some time in Greeley too. That's when things got serious.

I talked of moving her out to California. She said she couldn't leave the kids. I said okay, let's bring them along. She said she couldn't live with me with the kids there if we weren't married.

Do you see where this is going?

I think my hesitancy was fairly well justified. I had tried this marriage thing three times already, and hadn't had much luck making it work. I didn't have any trouble taking the blame for that, but was I ready to do it again?

Let me paint you a picture. I was a guy in my mid-40s, fairly successful in my chosen profession, sober (at least currently) and going to Grace Community Church. One of the major tenets of success in that church setting was the ability to support a family, to be a provider. Something I had failed at pretty miserably to date unless you count paying child support.

You might say I was staring at a reverse midlife crisis.

So I said okay.

I flew Maria out to Long Beach — met her with a Will You Marry Me? sign and everything. We visited Grace so she could see the children's and teens' ministries. I had asked a favor of my friend Joe Prevratil, the Queen Mary operator, to do the ceremony as captain of the ship, and Maria got excited.

I couldn't very well fit this family into my one-bedroom condo, so I went house hunting. Another friend, a City Councilman/real estate agent, had just the thing — a three-bedroom house with a

CHAPTER 34

big, fenced back yard and three big trees. It was in north Long Beach, but the neighborhood didn't look too bad, and I somehow managed to qualify for the mortgage.

As you can see, once a decision was made I jumped into it completely. I want things to be done — bad things happen if you wait, at least in my mind.

So just more than six months after that fateful Happy New Year call, I was reserving a U-Haul and a trailer for the move.

Oh, did I mention that this was a bit of a stress? I was working the whole time. And you know how I handled stress.

It was only a single drink now and then. Honest.

Chapter 35

I call it The Trip. Think "National Lampoon's Vacation" but in two days.

Ironically, there were parallels with my original move to California with the compatible one, some 10 years before. A U-Haul, a trailer pulling a car.

But that was about it.

I should have known I was in trouble when we traveled to the place I was supposed to pick up the U-Haul. They had a truck with a bench seat, as I had requested, but the thing had to be at least 30 years old.

The trailer was a little newer, and the brake lights actually worked, so away we went to load up.

Of course I was doing everything I could to save money, so the truck wasn't all that big. We loaded it up to the roof and still had plenty of stuff sitting on the ground.

So we pulled Maria's car onto the trailer and started loading it up. It was a predecessor to the soon-to-be-popular hatchbacks, so there was quite a bit of usable space. It too got loaded to the roof except for the driver's seat, where a 50-gallon aquarium full of fish and water took pride of place.

I have no clue what the final tonnage was, but I know it was quite a bit more than a 1960 box truck engine was rated for. But what the heck. I could do this thing.

I had to do this thing. That U-Haul was my version of a white horse and I was rescuing this family. Right?

The bench seat was required because it had to accommodate Maria, Charlotte and John in addition to me behind the wheel. All three of them were pretty skinny, so it wasn't a sardine can, but it

CHAPTER 35

wasn't stretching out on a sofa, either.

I had taken the Friday off to get to Greeley and get everything packed. I wanted to be back at work the following Monday, though, and after a day loading that meant a 48-hour window to cover the road from Greeley to Long Beach – 1,089 miles.

That's easily doable these days, especially since I typically drive 10-15 miles an hour above the speed limit. The Google map says it's 17 hours and change of driving.

But I wasn't going to be averaging any 70 miles an hour with this rig.

My plan was to get a very early start and make it to St. George, Utah, to spend the night with my father. That's southern Utah and only 90 minutes or so from Las Vegas. I figured we could have dinner with him if everything went as planned.

Wrong.

There are a couple of mountain ranges between Denver and California, as you might know. And it was early July.

We got the early start, and my passengers were back to sleep by the time I hit the first upgrade on I-70 outside Denver. It was slow going, but the truck kept chugging. It was only 7 a.m. and the temperature gauge barely moved.

Things were a little more concerning as I started up Loveland Pass – way up on the Great Divide. Loveland is the highest highway pass in Colorado, even if you take the Eisenhower Tunnel shortcut, which is at 11,112 feet in altitude. Maria and the kids were awake again as we crawled up the pass, and the temperature gauge was getting close to red when we made it to the tunnel.

We stopped when we got off the mountain to feed the kids, and the fish. At least that's what I told them – I was actually stopping to get water and let the truck cool down.

There's some very pretty country in that part of Colorado, and Glenwood Canyon is downright awe-inspiring. But when you're 14 and 11, scenery doesn't hold your attention for very long.

Charlotte and John were about as good as they could be. But

this was before iPhone games and the like. It was hot, and this truck didn't have air conditioning.

We soldiered on.

Grand Junction to Green River, Utah, is pretty flat high mountain desert, and we made up a little time there, but I was babying the truck to avoid overheating. We had quite a load. It was early evening by the time we crossed the border into Utah.

I was starting to worry a bit, but I tried to keep it to myself. I didn't have any stimulants beyond caffeine to help, and nothing to take the edge off the building stress. But I was being the manly man, and if the wagon trains could make it, so could we.

The kids were drowsy again when we headed out of Green River, which was a good thing. It was still hot, the next stretch of mountains were as steep as Loveland and the climb was a lot longer.

We barely made it to the first scenic viewpoint before I had to pull over to let the truck cool down. John was still awake enough to say "Is that smoke?" It was steam.

I won't say I panicked, but it was getting dark, and I knew how hard the climb was going to be. I pushed, and got back on the road. Too soon. The steam started again before the next pullout.

I've forgotten how many times we ended up stopping before we finally reached the crest and started across the mountain top. It was late, but it also was clear I couldn't push the truck for more speed.

I'd called Dad a couple of times to give him updates. Not going to make dinner. Go ahead and go to bed.

Then I started talking about driving straight through. There are a couple of serious climbs out of Las Vegas on the way to California, and I didn't think the truck would make it if we had to drive up them mid-day.

This did not thrill Maria, to say the least. She was worried about safety, to be sure, but she also knew her kids needed to stretch out for some real rest. John had already tried the floor on

CHAPTER 35

the passenger side of the cab.

She enlisted my father into the argument and they finally convinced me to stop, if just for a few hours, in St. George. We pulled into his driveway at 3 a.m., carried the kids inside and collapsed on the couch and recliner. I made Dad set an alarm for 6 a.m.

We were on the road again around 6:30, and the truck seemed to have a bit of new life. We made it through Vegas (no gambling this trip) and to the first serious hill by mid-morning.

It was very, very slow, but the temperature gauge stayed below red. What takes me less than 5 hours today by car took more than 12 hours that day – the Sunday traffic back to LA actually was a blessing because it forced me to go slow enough to keep from overheating.

We pulled up to the new house at twilight, went inside and slept on the floor. I'd worry about unloading later.

We were home.

Chapter 36

The next six weeks were a whirlwind. The house was built in 1947 and the previous owners had lived there for 30 or 40 years — until the husband died. Not surprisingly, there hadn't been many upgrades.

Maria had plans to work remotely, doing graphics work for the same outfit she had worked for in Greeley. But the house's wiring was still primarily knob-and-tube (a really old electrical wiring process with porcelain knobs acting as insulation), and had trouble handling the television, let alone a brace of computers.

Rewiring and adding a new power box was beyond me, so a contractor was required. That took a day or three.

Trying to make the kids happy with their rooms fell to Maria, and trying to keep Maria happy fell to me. That meant getting busy with wedding planning.

This would be my fourth wedding — a tally I'm not overly proud of. It was particularly scary considering my inability to make it into double digits with any of those marriages — heck, I didn't make it to five years with two of them.

But I did have a couple of things going for me with this one. Maria had been married before too, and was as motivated as I was to make this work. She was a woman of faith, I had the beginnings of a faith in God to lean on, and I was sober, for the most part.

I was riding my motorcycle to and from work, and it's hard to sneak a drink on a motorcycle. Trying to keep up with the newspaper, upgrading the house and planning the wedding kept me occupied.

For the most part, I was just trying to go with the flow. I liked

CHAPTER 36

being able to make Maria's dreams come true (still do), and I had managed to get fairly high credit limits on a couple of credit cards, so I just did it. We got a great deal on the Queen Mary for the wedding, thanks to John and Fran's connections and our friendship with Joe Prevratil. But I still had to pay for the reception, and we couldn't keep the guest list below 75 people.

I had to keep up appearances with the honeymoon plans, right? But I only had the weekend – had to work on Monday, you know.

So it was a helicopter trip to Catalina Island – a tourist destination 26 miles from Long Beach. The helicopter pad was next to the Queen, so I was literally able to whisk her away.

There were a few hiccups at the wedding, but for the most part everything was as it should be. Little John's sisters even managed to keep him standing sort of still and leave his tuxedo tie on until the "I do's" were said.

The reception was fine, too. I used sparkling cider for the toast even though it made me feel guilty allowing everyone to believe I was staying away from alcohol. (I did that day, but...)

Even the helicopter ride worked. It's only 20 or 30 minutes by air, and I was able to keep Maria occupied enough that her fear of heights didn't kick in.

We had a great honeymoon suite, with a nice view and a big bathtub. That was important because during our long-distance courtship, Maria would take a bubble bath after the kids were in bed while I talked to her by phone.

So she got her bubble bath on our wedding night. I had brought a bottle of champagne from the reception, and poured her a glass before I started reading the Song of Solomon, an amazingly seductive book in the Old Testament, aloud to her.

When I went back to the other room to pour her another glass of wine, you know I had to sample, just to make sure it was worthy.

It was only three or four swallows.

Chapter 37

We settled into the new family thing, trying to get the kids adjusted to Southern California life. They each had their own bedroom, and I had enough brains to avoid acting like I was their dad, at least at first.

Unless you have experienced it, I don't think I can explain what it's like to try to be a step-dad. Heck, I hadn't really had much experience being a dad, at least full time. Remember, Alex's mom took him away when he was 2 years old.

I pretty much left the discipline and adjustment thing to Maria. Looking back, it had to be really hard for both Charlotte and John – new schools, new friends, new everything. I used my connections to enroll them into their schools of choice and essentially crossed my fingers.

It was quite an adjustment for everyone, really.

Maria had been running the household on her own for a year or so. I had been living alone for longer. We had to adjust to living with each other, too.

I tried the "it's my house and I should be in control" approach, but that only lasted a few days, at least outwardly. I quickly took that attitude internal, where it caused plenty of resentment on my part, but kept the peace.

I handled it the way I handled most things back then. I buried myself in work. And yes, I had a baby bottle of wine, or a shot or two of peppermint schnapps, before I finally went home. It was just to mellow out. Really.

The world in general seemed unsettled after entering a new century. Another George Bush was running for President against Bill Clinton's vice president, Al Gore. The Y2K crisis was seemingly

CHAPTER 37

averted, but it felt like everyone was tiptoeing around.

We still were doing well at the *Grunion*. John and Fran kept the sales force focused on local business, particularly real estate, and our customer service kept the business owners happy.

That meant our newsroom was still well-staffed, including a proofreader that made us the envy of the folks at the *PT*, where misspellings and more were fairly common. The website was an afterthought – our audience was local, and they got the print edition for free, so they were happy.

My new situation as a family man kept my addiction under control. I occasionally got home with a slight buzz on, but made sure that there were no issues.

Maria had been a frequent churchgoer in Colorado, and we started attending Grace regularly. It was a 30-minute drive from our new home to Seal Beach, but it was worth it. At least I thought it was if it would keep the family together.

I even started taking the kids to Wednesday night youth groups. The high schooler, Charlotte, didn't always participate, but John got to play video games and foosball after the Bible study, so he was happy.

I had begun to think of myself as a Christian, but I didn't exactly delve into the study deeply. I'd like to think I was doing more than checking the church box, but in retrospect, it wasn't much more.

Christmas was upon us before we were really ready, but Maria managed. The holiday is a big deal for her, and we tried hard to meld some of our traditions together. She's a huge decorator.

Me? I went for the "buy their affection" route. I had paid off some of the credit card debt from the wedding, so I ratcheted it up again buying presents for Maria, Charlotte and John.

Of course it didn't work. They didn't seem to know how to respond and I got my feelings hurt when I felt I didn't get enough gratitude for my largesse.

Stupid.

◄ NO WALK IN THE PARK

And so it went. It wasn't bliss, but it wasn't bad, either. I wasn't Father Knows Best, but I didn't make too much trouble.

That spring we decided to get the kids a dog – I finally made a good decision! We had a big back yard, and we all had a background of having dogs in our lives.

The kids picked the dog at the Long Beach shelter, and gave him a name. Tiger was a Rottweiler-German Shepherd mix, eventually tipping the scale at around 100 pounds. He was the proverbial gentle giant with the kids and later a baby (a surrogate grandson). He sure made people pause though.

I have to admit, I kind of liked that.

Chapter 38

I should explain what I mean by a surrogate grandson. Daughter Aimee had made friends with a roommate at college, and that friend had become pregnant. The father wasn't around and Aimee and friend moved to Long Beach to prepare for the birth.

No way was Maria going to stay away from a baby in the making, even if the connection was one step removed. The girls lived fairly close to us in an apartment complex (I made the security deposit) and Maria could walk there, which she did frequently.

She made the walk more frequently after Erik's birth, trying to teach new mother all the old mother tricks. But it soon became clear that the new mother wasn't all that excited about being a mother.

New mother's parents lived up in L.A., and that grandmother took care of Erik when she could. Maria took charge when he was in Long Beach.

Erik was barely walking when his mother decided to change her approach to life – drugs, a girlfriend, an occasional wave to her kid. She bailed on the apartment (and the security deposit) and Erik started spending weekdays at L.A. grandparents' house.

We took him back to Long Beach most weekends, primarily to give L.A. grandparents a break. We soon became Grandma Maria and Grandpa Harry.

That routine continued literally for years. The L.A. grandparents filed for and received guardianship shortly after Erik started school. Erik's mom dropped in and out of his life sporadically.

It should come as no surprise that Erik was a troubled kid. He didn't do real well in school, despite efforts to get him tutoring, etc. The mother distanced herself further as she explored the wilder side of life.

NO WALK IN THE PARK

We continued the weekend visits, either going up to his soccer games or just picking him up and spending time with him in Long Beach. We included him in family outings and activities, with John acting as big brother.

By the time he reached high school, Erik had become a disciplinary problem, and was close to failing his classes. L.A. grandparents agreed with the school district that he should go to a "special" school designed to help students like him.

It sort of worked, and he did manage to wear his cap and gown. The diploma came a little later, but still…

L.A. grandfather had died a few years before, and L.A. grandmother was ready to retire. She wanted to get a van and take to the road – without Erik. None of his other blood relatives were able or willing to offer him a bed.

So he moved in with us. By that time John had moved on to the Marines, so there was a bedroom. He was there for more than three years before eventually moving to Colorado.

Sadly, his life has continued to be filled with drama – a girlfriend dying a tragic death, a debilitating work injury, etc. He's still hanging in there, and we're still his grandparents, even if there isn't any blood or legal connection.

We love Erik, surrogate or not.

Chapter 39

The *Press-Telegram* dates back to 1897, becoming the *Independent Press-Telegram* for a time. It survived a series of sales and mergers as a locally owned and operated publication. While that single-owner focus turned into part of a large publishing company with the sale of the paper to Ridder Publications in 1952, the Ridder family maintained the family-owned connection with a Ridder in Long Beach as publisher for decades.

But by the 1990s, the newspaper industry had begun changing in response to the ascendency of the Internet. Consolidations and cost-cutting were the new business model, led by a man named Dean Singleton. He built a media empire by purchasing struggling papers and gutting them, often firing entire staffs, then rehiring some reporters and editors at lower salaries to work for multiple papers.

In 1997, Singleton set his sights on Long Beach, purchasing the daily from what was by then Knight Ridder Inc. Following his proven business model, Singleton significantly reduced editorial staff, but left editorial control to the locals.

That staff still was significantly larger than my two reporters plus myself and a stable of freelancers. But we were able to provide better local coverage by continuing to focus solely on all the facets of Long Beach and its neighborhoods. John and Fran's advertising staff also outdid the daily consistently with a combination of personal customer service and a promise that readers saw their ads because the paper was read from start to finish.

While the *Press-Telegram* touted itself as the source for local news, they actually were operating as a regional paper. News from surrounding cities – Downey, Bellflower, Compton, Lakewood,

NO WALK IN THE PARK

Cerritos and more – competed for space on the front page.

There also were state and national stories throughout the paper in an attempt to make the *Press-Telegram* the only paper people needed. It certainly wasn't a competitor for the *Los Angeles Times* or the *Orange County Register*, though.

I took a similar approach of trying to be everything to everybody, just on a truly local level. It was my goal to have something in each *Grunion* for every type of reader. There were theater reviews, restaurant reviews, live entertainment reviews, a column about sailing and other water sports (called On The Water), business news and more.

By the turn of the century, we had established a reputation as a friend of both the arts and the nonprofits in Long Beach. I started a column called "For A Good Cause" to highlight events and fundraisers benefiting nonprofits, and we tried to have a "people" feature each week about the good work being done to help the less fortunate.

Still, my journalistic passion remained hard news in general, and political news in particular. John and Fran had established the idea that the *Grunion* would tell our readers what their civic leaders were doing and how it impacted them. I liked to think I doubled down on that approach, explaining the why and how behind the what, particularly in regards to government actions.

I'll admit to succumbing to that oh-so-competitive urge to scoop the competition by breaking a story first, but I also thought it critical that our stories explained the meaning or impact behind the actions we reported on.

In many ways, the *Grunion* became Long Beach's newspaper of record.

Another thing I established from the get-go was my personal column, called "A Pinch of Salt." John wrote a weekly column as well, which functioned as the paper's editorial voice more often than not.

Personal columns were not new, and the best (think Dave Barry in Florida or Steve Lopez in L.A.) drove readers to papers. I tried to bring my personal self to light in "A Pinch of Salt" too. My explanation for its existence was that I wanted readers to know that there were real people behind the newspaper, and that those people were involved in the community.

I would promote specific nonprofit activities in the column one week, then write about the dogs or the kids the next week. Some of the most popular columns seemed to be those where I talked about my fumbling attempts at Do-It-Yourself home projects, my family or my feelings.

The entire *Grunion* package was designed to fill a niche – the need people feel to know what's going on around them. It's called community newspapering, and I honestly believed that there would always be a need for such newspapers.

It would take more than two decades longer before I found myself questioning that concept.

Chapter 40

Maria and I made it through our first year without a lot of trauma. Her deal with the Colorado publication to do the graphics work remotely lasted for six months or so before the company cut ties. She began casting around for options.

There wasn't a whole lot of romance going on, what with two kids in the house. I put a lock on the bedroom door, but Maria couldn't get comfortable. I learned to live with it.

I'm pretty sure Maria knew I was drinking by our first anniversary, but I didn't bring it home, so it didn't seem to be a problem.

We got son John involved in AYSO soccer and he was doing okay at one of the better middle schools in the city (a 25-minute drive from the house). He made it clear he missed his dad, though. Charlotte was having trouble fitting in at high school, and had begun talking about how she could go back to Colorado.

In short, things were a bit tense at home.

But that certainly had little to do with what happened next.

Chapter 41

The telephone ringing woke me up at 6 a.m. on Tuesday, Sept. 11, 2001. My stomach dropped when I heard newspaper John's voice on the other end of the line. John never called me at home. I knew something was wrong.

"Turn on your television," is all John said.

You know what I saw – one of the Twin Towers in New York City burning. I watched the second plane hit the second tower and listened to the news about the Pentagon strike.

Tuesday was our editorial deadline day – most of the copy from outside writers came in that day in addition to the stories from the staff. I typically finished my own writing on Monday so I could handle it all.

That didn't matter. National newscasts were pointing to the Long Beach-Los Angeles port complex as a prime potential terrorist target – national news was suddenly local news.

I got to the office quickly and started making calls. My top assistant, Kurt Helin, went out to do on-the-ground coverage. The other full-timer, Amy Bentley-Smith, pitched in.

We were a small piece of the army of journalists numbering in the thousands nationwide obsessed with getting the news out about the most devastating attack on U.S. soil since Pearl Harbor. There were 2,996 deaths that day, and an uncounted number since then.

There were at least two big local stories – the response from government agencies and the local connections. Was anyone from Long Beach on the planes or in the Towers? How would our first responders handle it if the ports were attacked?

It's an understatement to say that our world changed that day, and not in a good way. We are still feeling the repercussions internationally, nationally and locally.

But that day, it was all about the immediate aftermath. It's hard for me to explain the adrenaline rush that accompanies chasing a huge story like this. It's about feeling like you are at the pinnacle of your craft, doing what you were meant to do.

Sure, the second-by-second coverage was on television and radio. But that just reinforced our mantra of local, local, local. Our readers wanted to know what it meant to them, what it meant to their neighbors and their town.

Since the attacks took place on Tuesday, that meant our Thursday newspaper would be timely — something that wasn't always the case being printed once a week. It also meant we were all going a hundred miles an hour Tuesday and production day Wednesday, when we pushed to get the very latest story possible in the paper.

We did a pretty amazing job, if I don't say so myself. And I mean all of us. John wrote what might have been his best column to date. Kurt, Amy and the rest of the crew gave it their all and then some. The advertising reps and the production crew did all they could to facilitate the latest possible news getting into print.

I was one proud editor when the *Grunion* began hitting porches on that Thursday morning.

Sadly, that would change in 12 short hours.

Chapter 42

The attack had been so sudden, many events scheduled that week were in limbo. One was the Long Beach Area Chamber of Commerce Golf Tournament, one of the bigger tournaments of the year, which long had been scheduled for Thursday, Sept. 13.

There were calls to carry on with normal life to "prove" that the terrorists had not shaken the United States. That was obviously untrue, but most of us did it anyway. That included the Long Beach Chamber.

I had an invitation to play and, after some discussion, it was decided I should wave the *Grunion* flag by participating. I think we teed off at 11 a.m.

This was back in the day when most golf tournaments were characterized by free-flowing booze on the course. Beer shared space with water and soda in ice tubs at virtually every hole, and more than one sponsor at the tee boxes included tequila shots with their freebies.

I decided early on that I would imbibe. I had earned it, after all. There were plenty of kudos on the course for the paper we had put out, along with plenty of talk about what the attacks would mean going forward.

The quality of my golf game, never great, deteriorated as the day went on. But with the exception of a few serious golfers intent on taking home another trophy, these tournaments are not designed to care about results. It's all about being with friends and having fun.

I was having fun. I wasn't the only one, but I was right up there with the lead pack.

A dinner and auction typically follow the round of golf at these tournaments, along with an open bar to help lubricate the potential auction bidders. I knew I couldn't stay – I had to pick up John and take him to soccer practice.

But a friend talked me into a last drink before I had to leave. I'll remember that last drink for a long time.

I was late to pick up John, so I just tossed my clubs in the trunk and got in the car without changing out of my golf shoes. I had driven home in golf shoes before; no big deal.

I thought I was driving carefully, and pulled into the turn lane going slowly. There was a pickup in front of me, waiting for the light to change.

I might have been going slowly, but I didn't stop until I had tapped the rear end of the truck. I honestly didn't think any damage had been done.

But the polite thing was to exchange insurance information. So I pulled around the corner behind them and stopped on a side street.

I wasn't fooling anyone this time. The couple in the truck clearly knew I was drunk, and had called the police. They stalled until the patrol car pulled around the corner.

Thirty minutes later I was in the back of that car, handcuffed and headed downtown.

Chapter 43

I had been editor of the *Grunion* for almost a decade, and thought I was fairly well known in Long Beach. My name didn't mean anything to the officers in the booking area, though.

I was polite, and followed directions – no need to make a bad situation worse.

Did I say bad? This was a disaster. There is a saying in AA that you need to find your bottom. Me in jail, for drinking then driving? That was lower than the bottom.

I was sure the entire city would be talking about it the next day. After all, the world revolved around me, didn't it?

My job was in jeopardy. My marriage was in jeopardy. My life as I knew it was in jeopardy.

After the fingerprints, the picture, giving up my possessions – including the laces from my golf shoes – I was escorted to the cell. I honestly couldn't tell you if there was anyone else in the cell, but it wasn't that big open space you see on some TV shows.

It was gloomy, and small. I spent the first hour or two feeling sorry for myself and bemoaning the situation I had put myself in. At least I wasn't blaming someone else. I knew who did this.

Eventually I calmed down enough to think about praying. I say "think about" because I was pretty sure I was so bad God didn't want anything to do with me.

But what option did I have?

I am far from the first person to ask God for help from behind bars. I'm far from the first to find His comfort either.

But I didn't pray that He would get me out of the trouble I was in. I prayed, over and over again, that He would take away the compulsion I had to drink.

NO WALK IN THE PARK

I had said that I was powerless over alcohol literally hundreds of times over the years in and out of AA meetings. I had also said hundreds of times that I believed in God and that Jesus had died to earn forgiveness for my sins.

It was different that night. No, I didn't see a light or hear a voice. But I did feel a peace. It felt like a weight had been lifted off me.

It was a miracle, even if I wasn't sure of it at the time. The compulsion was gone. God took it away.

That didn't mean everything was suddenly sweetness and light. I had to face the consequences of my actions. And they were heavy.

It had been determined that I was responsible for a collision with damage, which meant I had to post a bond to get out of jail. The only person I knew with the cash to post bail was my boss, John.

Worse, I had to ask Maria to ask him for the money, which meant telling Maria what I'd done. Remember, I was supposed to be picking up her son when I got arrested.

I was below humble. I was groveling. But she did what had to be done, and John came through, with my promise that he would be repaid on Monday.

He picked me up and took me home, pretty much without a word. I had Maria take me to a nearby convenience store so I could get a pack of cigarettes. We didn't talk either.

Chapter 44

As much as I might have liked it to happen, my life didn't stop.

Maria and I had planned a Vegas getaway that weekend. We had cheap flights, and decided to go – not for fun, but to talk with a couple of her friends.

Commercial flights had just resumed, but pretty much no one was flying. I think there might have been a dozen people on the plane going out, and the airport was essentially deserted.

We met Maria's friends at a coffee shop in one of the almost empty casinos. He was a preacher, or a past preacher, I don't recall. But he did have experience counseling alcoholics.

It was a good talk. I knew everything he had to say, but the reminders helped.

I don't remember much else about that trip. The guilt was overwhelming. I prayed for help finding a way through, finding a way to restore the trust I had destroyed.

First up was sitting down with Charlotte and John. There were lots of "I'm sorrys," and more than a few promises of "it will never happen again." It was the same discussion I had with Maria, more than once.

There was precious little reason for either Maria or the kids to believe me. Regaining any trust was going to take a lot of time, and the scrutiny would extend past the family and to the office – I was on probation with John and Fran, too.

The guilt and embarrassment I felt was at times overwhelming. But that wasn't the only reason I stayed far away from any form of alcohol.

There was no compulsion to drink. It wasn't fear of consequences (although that existed). I literally no longer wanted to feel the numbing effect I had sought so often in the past. God had taken it away.

Back in South Fork a decade before, when I earned my first DUI, I wrote a column about the experience. It was supposed to be a sort of public confession. I guess it was, although time proved the promise of reform empty and false.

There was no public confession this time around. I didn't even talk to the staff about it, although those interested in knowing undoubtedly found out. I was more focused on doing the work to make this no-drinking thing stick.

A good friend who was an attorney agreed to handle the legal end of things. He was and is a good attorney – I ended up with probation, a mandatory drinking and driving class and 90 days of AA meetings required.

This time around, I was paying attention. I found another AA group that was affiliated with my church, and became a semi-active participant. I asked a friend to be my sponsor, and worked the steps.

Making amends was the hardest part. It also was the most fulfilling. I had to admit to doing bad things, to acting hurtfully. But the apologies and pleas for forgiveness brought a peace to me as well.

I spent a good year walking on tiptoes around Maria and the kids. I spent the same amount of time avoiding any confrontation with Fran or John, while constantly trying to prove that I was sober in every way.

I made it through. Thanks to God.

Chapter 45

Through all the personal drama, I continued to function at the paper and in the community. I had been chair of the Public Corporation for the Arts board for a couple of years, leading efforts to get more money to support the arts – we even managed to get a one-time million-dollar windfall from the city.

But eight years on that board was enough. Beverly O'Neill was still mayor, and offered to appoint me to the Long Beach Parks and Recreation Commission.

This was a step into the big time, at least in our little pond. While the PCA was a quasi-governmental agency, this commission provided advice and oversight to the city's Parks, Recreation and Marine Department. It was created by the city's Charter and had specific responsibilities.

I had been a strong advocate for the arts in the paper while serving on the PCA, primarily through my column, but also in the editorial decisions about what would appear in the *Grunion*. We were the only paper in Long Beach to have a weekly theater review – always about the city's various live theater troupes. All about local, you know. We had a regular classical music column, and even tried a contemporary local music column for a while. Visual art also had a regular presence and its own columnist.

But aside from the drive to get more city money for the PCA, there was no real potential for conflict between my board role and my newspaper role.

Parks and Rec was a different situation. That commission weighed in on issues that could be controversial in the public – locations of parks, use fee policies and more. Often decisions were couched in the form of advice to the City Council, but there were situations where the commission had the final say, legally or practically.

So it was important to make sure people knew when I was wearing my *Grunion* editor hat and when I had put on my Commissioner hat. I avoided conflict of interest on the news pages by having one of my staff writers do stories involving the Parks, Recreation and Marine Department. When I wrote a column about parks or recreation issues, I said upfront that I was on the commission.

That convinced me – and John, I think – that we were being fair to all sides of the issues. When questions were asked about the paper's "objectivity," I argued that I could keep the issues separate. John supported me on that.

But there still were plenty of folks willing to criticize my perceived closeness with city officials and the city government. In hindsight, I think they might have had a point.

I say this after 25 consecutive years serving on three municipal commissions, chairing each for multiple years. For part of my tenure on Parks and Rec, and for my entire eight years as a Water Commissioner, I was literally on the city's payroll, receiving a monthly stipend.

And I will continue to argue that we provided fair coverage of those departments and the city as a whole during that time. When the city did something wrong, or city politicians offered questionable opinions, we wrote about it.

But. One of my mantras when working with boards and non-profit organizations is that perception is reality in the public's eye. And with the benefit of time away, I can understand the perception that I couldn't be "objective."

Some of the criticism of my city work came from other news outlets, where they see their role as watchdogs, always on the lookout for maleficence at city hall. A couple of those publications took it further, with a stated belief that the city employees and elected officials were the enemy, always doing the wrong thing.

CHAPTER 45

In some ways, I blame Woodward and Bernstein for that attitude. Young journalists see the road to fame as breaking the next Watergate scandal, and that requires a certain state of mind.

I cannot accept that. I have operated and led the *Grunion* with the philosophy that we are here to make our community a better place. I also happen to believe that most Long Beach leaders, both elected and appointed, have that goal in mind as well.

There certainly are some politicians with personal agendas, whether that's money, a higher position or power. But most of those folks are pretty blatant in their efforts. Then reality becomes the perception.

I've been accused of being a municipal cheerleader. If that means working for the betterment of my community, I'll live with that.

I honestly think that's what God kept me around to do.

Chapter 46

As I worked my way through the aftermath of the DUI, I found myself getting closer to God.

To begin with, I really didn't have any desire to drink – after years of thinking about nothing else. No doubt that had something to do with fear of consequences, both legal and personal.

But I became more and more convinced that God had answered my prayer to take the compulsion away. How else could I explain the absence of a physical craving that had driven my actions for the last 30 years?

I leaned on my church and the family at Grace. When my lawyer friend said I needed to have two people come in to vouch for my character, I asked the associate pastor and a church elder friend to step up – they did so without hesitation. I think it was a matter of it being the Christian thing to do.

As I've mentioned, I joined an AA group being hosted by the church. For several months, I also saw a faith-based psychologist recommended by the church.

Somewhere in there, I decided to get baptized in front of the church. I had been baptized as an infant in the Catholic Church, but our denomination believes in baptism chosen by the individual as an expression of accepting Jesus as our savior.

That typically meant middle school students. I was 47. But it was meaningful to me. It really felt like a symbol that I was born again, a new being in Christ.

That Sunday, I truly felt like I was a Christian. I've felt that way ever since.

It wasn't all sweetness and light. There were still bouts of depression in regards to my situation, and frustration when Maria

CHAPTER 46

or the Blowitzes didn't immediately trust that I was on a new path.

Some of it was physical. The detox process took much longer than the first couple of nights of the shakes. I felt on edge and defensive for several months.

More of it was mental. I had been raised on a diet of guilt – it was the primary motivational tool used by my mother, who learned it from the Catholic Church.

I could not shake the knowledge that I had done wrong, and couldn't understand how God could forgive and accept me with those actions sitting there on my report card. Heck, I didn't believe that confession and a few Hail Marys or Our Fathers could absolve my guilt when I was 10 – how could I reconcile a forgiving God without that?

I'm still working on that one 25 years later.

But it was time for another miracle.

Chapter 47

Maria and I had discovered that working on our 50-plus-year-old house was a good way to work off any tension in the air. I had already transformed the drop-down ironing board in the kitchen into a spice rack, and we'd done quite a bit of decorating the kids' bedrooms. There was lots going on in the yards as well.

I have no doubt that the wall-to-wall carpet everywhere except the kitchen and bathroom was great and stylish when it was installed. But it was a new century, and we had discovered there was hardwood flooring under that carpet.

I'd like to say we were young and naive, but I was just naive. We decided to tear out the carpet and refinish the hardwood. And we were going to do it ourselves.

I gained great respect for carpet-layers in the next couple of weeks. That carpet was meant to stay where they put it.

Tearing it out was mostly brute strength — I still had a little of that back then. Once the rug and the tack strips were gone, we started the process of bringing the hardwood back to life.

That involved treating the wood, buffing it with an industrial buffer, then doing it all over again. It probably comes as no surprise that Maria and I did most of the work — son John wasn't too interested in how the floors looked. He could just cover it with clothes, after all.

Little by little, the job progressed. We had rented the buffer, so we worked pretty long and hard to get that part done.

I thought we were close when we stopped for the night. We collapsed into bed.

The pain woke me up about 2 a.m. High in the chest, and sharp. I tried to get up, intending to get some aspirin. That was a no go.

CHAPTER 47

Shaking Maria awake, I told her we needed to go to the hospital, and she was going to have to drive. The pain wasn't stopping. But I never thought about calling 911 – something my firefighter buddies later gave me a hard time about.

Long Beach Memorial Medical Center was a few miles away, and I knew they had a good heart program thanks to our Valentine's Date Night and stories I had done. We made it to the emergency room, and they took me in right away.

When the nitroglycerin didn't impact the pain, they called the cardiologist on duty that night. Then they gave me something stronger for the pain, and the rest of the night became a bit of a blur.

It was a heart attack, but clearly not of the "widow-maker" variety. The cardiologist had put in a stent to open a blocked artery and came by the next day to give me directions and discharge me from the hospital.

No, I'm not talking about surviving the heart attack as the miracle, although Maria might beg to differ. The miracle came as they put me in the wheelchair to go to the car, and the doctor offered a prescription for a nicotine patch.

I told him I didn't think I needed it.

If you recall, my parents smoked like chimneys, and I started when I was 17 years old. I became a two-pack-a-day Marlboro man early in my 20s.

I had quit smoking plenty of times. But my high drug tolerance extended to nicotine – I could wear a patch, chew Nicorette and smoke a cigarette all at the same time. I blamed it on the stress of the job.

But as I was leaving the hospital, I knew that I was done smoking. God had given me the warning, then taken that addiction away, too.

I haven't had a cigarette since that day.

It really is a miracle.

The heart disease didn't disappear, though. Five years later, I was back for another stent. And five years after that, I recognized

◀ NO WALK IN THE PARK

the symptoms and made plans for a few sick days to get the third stent.

When the pain started up again six years later, I figured I'd get the fourth stent and that would be the end of it. Only after they did the angiogram, the doc said it was time for more drastic action. Open heart surgery was needed, and would happen within a week.

I'll tell you more about that later.

But for now, just remember the miracles of recovery – from alcohol and from nicotine.

Thank you God.

Chapter 48

So here I was, a baby Christian with no alcohol, no cigarettes, and little to no sex.

If you know anyone who has recently become a Christian as an adult, you know that the excitement can cause some over-the-top reactions. Remember that I was a pretty public person due to my position – and my column in particular.

I had made it a rule to be open in "A Pinch of Salt," and I had a hard-earned reputation for telling it like it was, at least from my perspective. So it probably comes as no surprise that I decided to write a column about my faith.

As the executive editor of the *Grunion*, I was the last line of editing for pretty much everything that went to print, including my own stories. The exception was the opinion page. John and I had agreed long ago that we would read each other's columns but not change them except for grammar and punctuation. If there was an issue, we'd talk about it.

We talked about this one. A lot.

John was concerned that my evangelical fervor would alienate our predominantly liberal readership. He said he was okay with talking about faith, but wanted me to tone it down.

At one point, we literally counted the number of times I had written the word God in the column. I guess it was supposed to be some sort of bargaining point.

I was not the best at accepting criticism or being challenged, especially when it came to my writing. Add the passion of the newly born again, and the discussion soon threatened to turn into an all-out battle.

Fortunately, I had a couple of places where I could let off

steam about the issue. One was a Bible study that was as much an accountability group as a study.

I fully expected total support for my position when I told the group about the "how many Gods can I have" debate. But my friend Bob, the leader of the group, reined me in.

He suggested that a full-on frontal assault might not be the best way to let my readers know about my conversion. He agreed that the number of times I said God was pretty irrelevant, but suggested that John's position of moderation made perfect sense – especially since he was the owner!

I took the advice and went back to John with a compromise and an apology. Going forward, I was much more careful about how I shared my faith – but I did share it. In fact, mentions of faith became more frequent over the years, but hopefully more subtle.

I call it guerilla evangelism.

There was another visible manifestation of my changes in personality and faith I found interesting. I decided to stop cursing. Not just stopping the taking of the Lord's name in vain, but the whole litany of vulgar words. The F-word had always bothered Maria, and it became an emphasis for me.

For most of my life, I could cuss with the best of them. I had my heavy construction days as training, along with the locker room life. So this was a pretty big change.

I don't remember making an issue of it in the office – maybe a sour face when one of the production crew let fly. Still, it wasn't long before the cursing subsided, at least when I was around.

Was that a good influence? A Christian approach? I like to think so.

Chapter 49

Another impact from my growing in the faith was an increasing conviction that I needed to give back. We already were doing a lot in the papers for the nonprofit community by writing stories about them, and I ramped it up by writing columns.

I liked to talk about how special events raised money for good causes while the donors had a good time. But I couldn't write about every charity event, and I wanted to give them a little more play than a one-sentence calendar listing.

So "For A Good Cause" was born. There could be a paragraph about every fund-raising event in the city happening in the coming week or two. I had one of the staffers compile it; FAGC, as we called it, was a hit, both with readers and nonprofits.

We had to take care of our advertising customers too, so at Fran and John's request we started the "Business Beat" feature about the same time. I have to admit it did take some pressure off me when a restaurant launched a new menu, or a business had its sixth anniversary sale, and the owner thought it was big news.

Something for everyone, right?

But that was just doing my job. My service on the Chamber Board, even the Parks and Rec Commission, was at least partially about waving the *Grunion* flag.

So I started looking around for nonprofits where my board experience and connections could make a difference.

God heard me. Just a couple of weeks after I began looking, there was a Mission Moment at Grace about Precious Lamb Preschool. One of the church members, Sharalyn Shaw-Croft, had started the preschool.

The preschool was for homeless children, and was free to attend.

The idea was to give the parents time to work on getting their lives back on track. Whether it was attending rehab or conducting job searches, those were impossible tasks with a 3- or 4-year-old on your hip.

Sharalyn had promised a Christ-based mission, and had delivered. At the end of the presentation, there was a call for people interested in serving as board members.

I raised my hand.

That was the beginning. I had written stories about domestic violence in both Greeley and Long Beach. WomenShelter of Long Beach was in the center of downtown, and had a rescue shelter in addition to providing a hotline, counseling services and more.

Then-Executive Director TuLynn Smylie asked me to lunch to talk me into joining their board. I would have said yes if she had just called. It was a cause I could get behind.

I had worked with a fascinating woman named Janet McCarthy while we served together on the Chamber of Commerce board. She was the president and CEO of Goodwill Serving the people of Southern Los Angeles County, headquartered in Long Beach.

She and I stepped down from the Chamber board at about the same time. Almost immediately, she asked me to join her board. I loved Goodwill's "a hand up, not a hand out" philosophy, and their use of store revenue to support their workforce training programs and other services. I signed on.

Each of these organizations were different, with different needs. They were all good about not just keeping me around in hopes of free publicity. I think I contributed to their success here and there.

I haven't tried to keep to a strict chronology here, but there were a number of years when I was on all three of these nonprofit boards as well as either the Parks and Rec Commission or the Water Commission.

It was the Christian thing to do.

In 2013, I was scheduled to become chair of both the Goodwill board and the Water Commission. I had stepped off the

CHAPTER 49

WomenShelter board and decided to leave Precious Lamb as well to lighten the load. But I continue to support them both to this day.

I was blessed to have the *Grunion* platform for more than 30 years, and WomenShelter was a beneficiary of that partnership. In 2004, we began a holiday gift card drive to benefit the victims of domestic violence and their children who were being served by WomenShelter.

Like the newspaper, the drive started small, grew and fell. But it took place again last year, and raised another $30,000. That brought the total to more than $350,000 in two decades.

Chapter 50

As I've said, it was part of my job as the executive editor to represent the newspaper at social events. I won't lie – it's a great perk. It helped that Maria enjoys those galas and events, too.

But there is a problem. Much like those charity golf tournaments I like to play, the booze usually flows freely – in both senses of the word.

Who was I to turn down a free drink? When I was drinking, these events were something I looked forward to.

But becoming a hermit so I didn't have to face alcohol was not an option with the job I had. It was up to me to be strong and show some character, right?

Wrong. I leaned on God, praying before events to remind me what kind of path I would be on with just one drink.

Maria enjoys a glass of wine, even an occasional cocktail, at these events. I discovered that a tonic water with a twist of lime looks just like a gin and tonic in the glass, so I could drink along with her without the extended explanations of why I wasn't drinking.

Seriously, that was a thing. Attitudes have changed significantly over the last two decades, and the to-drink-or-not-to-drink discussion seldom comes up today.

But back in the day, it was a pretty big deal. If someone asked if they could get you a drink and you said no, it could be taken as an insult.

There was some pride involved. "What, you don't drink so you're better than me?"

Don't say yes to that.

The best response I've been able to come up with is "I got my fill earlier in life." That tells them you are a recovering alcoholic without telling them you're a recovering alcoholic. It puts the judgment on me, not them.

AA old-timers will tell you to just stay out of the situation in the first place. Don't go to bars for business meetings, don't go to picnics you know are thin excuses for keggers.

Good advice. As I said, it doesn't work in my situation. Instead, longevity in sobriety has allowed me to not even think about it anymore.

I pour Maria a glass of wine with a steady hand, and no judgment. Thank you, God.

Chapter 51

Timing is everything in business, and John and Fran were experts in both timing and business. It was 2004 and our "local first, last and always" philosophy was working well in terms of both news coverage and retail advertising sales.

But if you looked carefully, you could see things beginning to slip. I mentioned how the Web-based Craigslist had made inroads in our classified advertising. A website called Monster broke new ground with online job searches. Craigslist expanded from sales to include apartment rentals.

We were kicking the *Press-Telegram*'s butt in local advertising, and holding our own with coverage as well. The free home-delivery model John and Fran had used from the beginning continued to pay off as we expanded circulation and coverage area. I don't recall the exact number, but we had to be producing more than 60,000 copies a week when you combined the *Grunion* and the *Downtown Gazettes*, and most of those newspapers were delivered to individual homes.

In other words, the *Gazette* probably was at its peak value. A few of the longer-tenured employees, including me, had talked about buying the paper a couple of years before. But we couldn't come anywhere close to even a significant down payment, let alone enough cash to convince John and Fran to sell.

There was someone with enough cash, though. Our friend, Mr. Singleton.

Singleton had been buying and selling papers all across the country for nearly three decades. A couple of its biggest purchases were the *Houston Post* and the *Denver Post*.

In the early 2000s, the Media News corporate entity flirted with

CHAPTER 51

bankruptcy on and off. It appears from its history that Singleton and his partners sold some papers in order to keep others.

He had kept all his Los Angeles-area properties, including the *Los Angeles Daily News*, and the *Press-Telegram*.

Singleton came to Long Beach from his Denver headquarters in January 2004 to announce the *Grunion* purchase personally. John and Fran ushered him into the *Grunion* offices on a Monday morning, around the time we usually had the weekly staff meeting.

The news of the sale was a surprise, but not really a shock. John and Fran had owned the paper since 1981, building it from a glorified neighborhood newsletter to an influential weekly newspaper in one of the largest cities in California. And the timing – the purchase price was kept private, of course, but there was no denial when it was asked if the price reached eight figures.

John and Fran took care of their core employees in the deal. We didn't get a percentage, but we did all get a significant "goodbye" check, and there was no question that we all still had jobs – unlike what happened when the *Press-Telegram* was purchased.

In fact, they had somehow managed to get Singleton to promise that he or his company would not change the editorial approach for five years after the paper changed hands. I've never heard of that caveat in a deal before or since. But it was huge, especially for me, because I retained editorial control.

I will forever be in John and Fran's debt for that.

I don't remember much of what Singleton said that morning. But one comment was worth a whole bunch of those newspaper awards we won over the years.

"We couldn't beat ya," Singleton said. "So I bought ya."

Chapter 52

The transition actually went fairly smoothly. I did a story on the sale, as did the *Press-Telegram*, but the wall remained up in terms of competition for both advertising and stories, just as promised.

Yes, they did bring in a company man to be the publisher, and no doubt he had a number to hit to please the corporate bosses. But he was a pretty laid-back guy (he had been in Alaska before Long Beach, I believe) and took the "if it ain't broke, don't fix it" approach.

After a month or two, I don't think anyone in town even remembered that we were owned by the same company. That made a difference – people develop loyalty to a paper much like they do for high schools.

The folks who swore by the *Grunion* loved to bad-mouth the *P-T*. It might have worked the other way, too, but I didn't hear that end of the conversation.

By this time, I had intertwined my personality with the newspaper. I was only half-kidding when I proclaimed that "I am the *Grunion*." I know that must have upset John and Fran, and I did indeed know that the paper was the product of a very talented team. (In fact, a few years later we did a promotion campaign where everyone on staff was filmed saying "I am the *Grunion*.")

But there was little doubt that I was the face of the paper, particularly after John and Fran departed. It was very, very easy to fall into the trap of ego, whether I was in the general public or sitting on a board or a commission.

The default was that everything was all about me, failures as well as successes.

CHAPTER 52

Looking back, I have no idea how I made it through that period without falling back into drinking. I can only turn to my growing faith in God.

Maria and I had started attending a couple's group at church, and that helped us through a lot. Charlotte had convinced Maria to let her go back to Colorado to finish high school with her friends.

John and I battled through his adolescence; I was totally clueless about how to help him. The church youth group helped for a while, then it didn't – although they kept trying.

We did experience a church thing together that I found extremely convicting. It was in October the fall before the *Grunion* sold.

Our church had been contacted by an outfit called Baja Ministries, which coordinated trips into Mexico to build houses for the poor. I had made one trip before by myself, but this time I was driving and bringing Maria and John.

Our destination was outside Tecate, a slum on a hill a few miles east of Tijuana. There were several thousand families housed in shacks, often made of garage doors, sheet metal and tarps. No running water, and bare wires stealing electricity from power lines running down every other dirt street.

There were about 40 of us from church in vehicles packed with supplies, clothing and such. Maria was part of the group planning to do a children's ministry; John was with me on the house construction team.

Baja Ministries provided a concrete slab and the construction material. They had the thing down to a science – an actual building with a roof, walls and wiring (no plumbing, but a new outhouse) could be built in a weekend.

We were welcomed with open arms. I managed to help put up a few walls, pound a few nails and paint a spot or two.

I also managed to make a spectacle of myself, sliding down the plywood roof and falling to the ground 8 feet below. The doc on our team opined my head was hard enough I likely didn't get a concussion, and I was back to work an hour later – bruised, battered and humbled, but standing upright. (I didn't go back on the roof.)

Walking away from the fall was, I suppose, a bit of a miracle. But the presence of God I experienced that weekend was truly found in the people living in that slum. They were so grateful for everything, from the potato salad and barbecued chicken we served for lunch to the chance to play a game with their children.

Some of us stopped long enough Sunday to join their hour of worship. It was, of course, in Spanish, but I could literally feel the joy of their faith in God's presence.

I wrote one of my more popular columns about that trip, and I still think of those people today. Can I ever be as thankful as Ramon and Sophia were when they received the keys to their home? I know I should be. I try.

Thanks for the experience, God.

Chapter 53

The city of Long Beach continued to suffer from tough financial times, with city budget debates characterized by what to cut where. But the business economy was holding its own, the real estate market in particular.

That was good news for the *Grunion*. While our classified ad section continued to shrink, our display advertising remained strong. Papers were routinely 48 pages or more, and the profitability of our bottom line kept the corporate office from cutting our payroll.

One of the big events, at least in Long Beach, took place in 2006. That was when Beverly O'Neill stepped down after serving as mayor for 12 years.

Beverly had come from nowhere – well, she had been president/superintendent of Long Beach City College, so that's somewhere – to get elected in 1994. Beverly had no public political experience, though. She had to deal with the closure of the U.S. Naval Shipyard and the Navy's departure, spending much of her first two terms in office reshaping the city's economic base.

Then she went and decided to run for a third term as a write-in candidate. Long Beach's charter at the time limited the mayor and council to two terms on the ballot. It meant that Beverly had to win without her name on the ballot both in the primary and the general election.

She did it, and did it easily. The big campaign push was giving out pencils with her name on them so people would spell her name correctly. Her election was national news – the first-ever big city mayor to win as a write-in.

Beverly wasn't universally loved in Long Beach, but almost.

She had cultivated a leadership style of unfailing public politeness and caring, while getting things done behind the scenes.

I had become an unabashed fan – although I could and did still take her on in policy matters.

What most impressed me, and plenty of other observers, was her honest love for Long Beach and desire to serve solely to make her city better.

Lots of politicians start their careers by saying they are only interested in serving their community, then quickly find ways to climb the ladder of political success. In this age of term limits, that's pretty much the only way to become a career politician.

That's not necessarily a bad thing, as a few good representatives for Long Beach have proven over the years. The prototype was Alan Lowenthal, who went from being a City Councilman to a state Assemblyman to a state Senator to a 10-year stint as Long Beach's representative in Congress. He always made his constituents the priority.

That path wasn't for Beverly, though. She could have won election to any office in Long Beach, state or federal. She likely would have been a force if she had run for a statewide office.

I asked her why she didn't do just that. She told me she didn't want to leave Long Beach. The idea of living even part-time in Sacramento or Washington D.C. held no appeal.

Beverly ultimately became one of the most important people in my life. I started lobbying her to let me write her biography within a year of her leaving office. It took more than three years to convince her to at least consider it.

Her public life was quite the story in itself. But I was more intrigued by what shaped the leader that Beverly became.

It was all about alcoholism.

Beverly's father was a problem drinker in her early years – so much so that her mother, Flossie Lewis, had to provide for the family. It was a tough time for them.

But there was a light at the end of the tunnel. Flossie discovered

CHAPTER 53

a new group just forming in Long Beach called Alcoholics Anonymous. She took her husband by the hand and got him to go to a few meetings.

It took a few tries, but the approach finally worked. Beverly's dad got sober, and he and Flossie were central figures in establishing both AA and Al-Anon – the group for family members of alcoholics – in Long Beach. For several years, their home acted as the city's AA central office and Beverly had consistent involvement in the program.

That experience, along with a solid grounding in church, made Beverly the leader she became.

I know, because she told me so.

Not a bad role model.

The book was published in 2010. It's called "Passionately Positive: The Beverly O'Neill Story," and it did pretty well – in Long Beach at least.

Chapter 54

In addition to the alcoholism recovery connection, I found compelling Beverly's passion for helping Long Beach become a better place. I wanted to make a difference like that, too.

In an early talk with one of my mentors, Joe Prevratil (several years before he presided at my wedding), I had a moment of candor, telling him that I wanted to be a person of substance in Long Beach. I wanted to be a mover and shaker, and I wanted people to know it.

That ego-driven approach was my own little secret – but I didn't hesitate to point out my service on city commissions and the difference it made.

I've already mentioned the "I am the *Grunion*" attitude, and that newspaper platform gave me a pretty loud voice. I didn't hesitate to use it.

Here's a little secret. Newspaper writers do the job for the love of the work, but that name at the top of the story is a pretty powerful motivator, too. That byline is as good as a payday, especially for young reporters.

Lots of journalists are enamored with the idea of being a watchdog. Speaking truth to power is a popular phrase, and uncovering malfeasance is the Holy Grail for many reporters. Questioning motives and rationale of politicians, business leaders and the like is a time-honored tradition for the press.

I'm in full support of that approach. But all too often that requires an adversarial attitude, leading to a belief that all government action is questionable and all political motives are self-centered.

Over the years, I built my credibility on being able to see the good as well as the bad. And despite talking often about my cynicism as a curmudgeonly old newspaper guy, I typically believed

CHAPTER 54

the best about someone – at least until they proved otherwise.

Beverly was a good example of that. I kept waiting for the dark side to show, and I never saw it. Some of her enemies made the claim she was too good to be true. But her actions only proved the veracity of her words.

That extended past her government role to her private life. She strongly supported the many nonprofit organizations that call Long Beach home – after leaving City Hall she hosted a public access television show called Heart of the City spotlighting one or two service organizations every week.

Just as she started me on my civic service by appointing me to boards, her passion for the nonprofit sector pointed me toward helping them. I used the *Grunion* to give them a larger presence in the community, particularly when they had an event. I used my Pinch of Salt personal column to advocate for them. When I was asked to join a board, I said yes.

I always prefaced my acceptance by letting them know I didn't have money to donate. John and Fran had treated me well, at least comparatively speaking, but newspapering is not the career for getting rich. I carried a balance on credit cards because I had a hard time saying no, and we were essentially living paycheck to paycheck. My first priority had to be providing for my family.

There's a well-worn phrase about what nonprofits look for from board members. They want your time, talent and treasure. (I add your contacts to that list.)

I had no treasure, and I hated to ask for money. But I could and did spend my time and tried to use my talents attempting to help. Soon enough, those talents included helping boards work efficiently and making the connections necessary to create partnerships.

For the last 20-plus years, I've always found myself serving on five or more boards, commissions or committees at the same time.

Hi. My name is Harry and I'm a workaholic. That's an addiction I haven't been able to shake.

Chapter 55

We managed to keep producing a well-read, informative and profitable set of newspapers through the middle of that first decade of the 2000s. We even collaborated with a community initiative to connect neighborhoods along transportation corridors by launching the *Uptown Gazette* in 2008. It was a replated version of the *Downtown Gazette* with front page news focused on the north Long Beach neighborhoods including California Heights, Bixby Knolls and Virginia Country Club. The process was exactly what I had done in the *South Fork Tines-Mineral County Miner* days.

It was partially financed by a grant from the Knight-Ridder Foundation. The Ridders stayed involved with Long Beach even though they no longer owned the *Press-Telegram*. If you look around and see how local news outlets are trying to compete today, you'll see that they were ahead of their time with the nonprofit support.

Then the Great Recession hit.

There were some early signs it was coming – the housing bubble had burst, with prices falling quickly and sub-prime loans being abandoned. Then the recession began in earnest in December 2007 – even if we didn't know it until the middle of 2008.

What, you might ask, does a recession have to do with the newspaper business? Start with the definition of a recession – "An overall decline in economic activity mainly observed as a slowdown in output and employment." – Oxford Reference Dictionary.

Businesses of all shapes and sizes saw sales decline. For the *Grunion*, the most important sectors were restaurants and the beauty/health industry – places where people spent discretionary income.

CHAPTER 55

It's a well-known marketing school fact that when things get tough, the first thing most businesses cut is advertising. We argued that advertising was even more important in a downturn in order to attract what few customers might be out there – another marketing school dictum. That worked about as well as you might expect when talking to struggling business owners – not at all.

By the time the Great Recession limped to an end around July 2009, the *Grunion* had shrank by a good 16 to 20 pages. The number of pages are determined by the number and size of display ads, and there weren't many of those left.

Ironically, the industry that had started the whole thing with the housing market collapse, the real estate industry, kept the *Grunion* afloat during much of that time. There were fewer and smaller real estate ads, to be sure, but the medium- to high-end market most of our advertisers served wasn't hit as badly as the general housing world.

Remember that we were now part of the journalism conglomerate called Media News. Singleton's model with that company was to cut and consolidate jobs so reporters and other positions were shared among papers.

And the deal that Singleton had made to leave the *Grunion* alone for five years after the sale had ended.

You have to give them credit; the top brass responded quickly once the recession hit. We stopped filling vacancies early in 2008. Then the matching for our 401Ks stopped. Then management (including me) took a "voluntary" salary cut that magically was the same size as the raise I had received a few years before.

By the end of the Great Recession, when I did get a begrudging okay to fill a position, I was limited to offering entry-level pay. That shrunk the talent pool significantly.

One of the joys of the executive editor job was helping young journalists grow in their skills and experience, then watching them advance their careers. I was blessed to have several successes in that regard.

NO WALK IN THE PARK

But I also had a couple of real disasters. When that happens, you just have to shrug it off and try again, which is what I did. If I could get the corporate office to let me fill the position, that is.

We survived the Great Recession and turned the page to the 2010s. But it's no exaggeration to say that we were a shadow of our former selves.

Chapter 56

It would be a disservice if I didn't tell you about the appointment of Simon Grieve as the *Grunion* publisher in 2007, shortly before the Great Recession. Simon had come on board before John and Fran sold, working as the marketing manager. He had taken over sales of the real estate advertising by the time the publisher spot opened up.

I threw my hat in the ring as well. I felt compelled to do it in order to protect the integrity of the *Grunion*.

But it was clear to everyone, including me (as my interview showed), that I didn't have the skill set for this job. I couldn't sell my way out of a paper bag, and I had no desire to give up the editorial end.

Simon still had to report to the higher-ups just like the two company publishers Media News had tried out before him. But he was part of the *Grunion* team, understood the community philosophy and was ready to defend our paper. And they liked the fact that he handled the real estate advertising, too.

In the county just south of Long Beach, the owners of the *Orange County Register* were struggling, eventually declaring bankruptcy. When Freedom Communications, the company that owned the *Register* and a few other publications, came out of bankruptcy, it was with several Wall Street investment firms taking control – including Alden Global Capital. Remember that name.

In July 2012, Boston multi-millionaire Aaron Kushner and his partner Eric Spitz bought Freedom Communications and the *Register* for $50 million. Kushner made a splash with an expansion plan he said would save newspapers, in direct opposition to the cost-cutting measures most publishers were taking.

He more than doubled the size of the *Register* newsroom to more than 400 employees – far more than the *Los Angeles Times*. He focused on the print product, increasing sections, adding magazines and more, instead of worrying about the news battle taking place online.

I, along with most of the working journalists I knew, were cheering him on. This was the model we grew up with, after all. And look at all those new jobs!

But he was pressuring what by then had become the Southern California News Group, which included the *Press-Telegram*, the *Los Angeles Daily News* and us, among others. When Kushner bought the daily *Press Enterprise* in Riverside in November 2012, SCNG management got nervous.

It was all out of my sphere of influence – above my pay grade – so I didn't worry about it. It didn't impact me, right?

Until Kushner decided to open the *Long Beach Register* in August 2013, thinking he could take over the town. Now there were problems.

Chapter 57

Kushner came into Long Beach aggressively, pretty much like he did everything. He hired away a couple of *Press-Telegram* reporters, and trumpeted that he was going to really cover local Long Beach news – as if we weren't already doing that.

I was summoned to the *Press-Telegram* office for a strategy session. It was more like a war council, with the 5-star general CEO of SCNG coming down to give us our marching orders.

The strategy included a marketing campaign that made it clear what had been true since the purchase nearly a decade ago – the *Grunion* was part of the *Press-Telegram*. The *Grunion* was still all locally-produced news, and the *Press-Telegram* would begin using our stories to be more local. Together, we could claim to be super local – unlike the *Register*.

That meant that I was supposed to use stories from *Press-Telegram* writers in the *Grunion*, too. I'll admit that I wasn't thrilled – the *Grunion* had been filled by me and my staff for more than 20 years.

But we were united against a common enemy. I did what I had to do.

This was the first time in my career that I had a direct competitor for my turf. While it had been fun to beat the *Press-Telegram* newsroom, they had never been the enemy. The *Long Beach Register* was literally calling us out.

So I put my back into it. I made sure all my contacts in city government, local nonprofits and elsewhere knew that I was still here to tell their stories, and get it right. I had a couple of decades of institutional history and proven credibility in my pocket.

On the other hand, the *Register* team were interlopers. The

Press-Telegram folks who defected to the other team lost a lot of credibility.

The *Long Beach Register* started out as a daily paper, ostensibly competing against the *Press-Telegram*. But week after week, the *Grunion* had at least one and usually more stories that the *Register* didn't even know about.

The difference? We had boots on the ground. People called us with tips; I knew where to look for stories and knew when they might happen.

So the *Register* was getting beaten consistently on the editorial side. The same was true on the advertising front. Even with the discounts you might expect from a startup and pushing Orange County ads into the Long Beach paper, they couldn't keep up with the *Grunion*, let alone the *Press-Telegram*.

In the meantime, Kushner was hemorrhaging money. As much as the newspaper world liked the emphasis on print newspapers and lots of editorial jobs, there was a reason the new online, cost-cutting model dominated the industry. Expenses there were less by a factor of 10 than producing a print edition.

In hindsight, it was a bit of a last gasp for the old-school newspaper approach. It quickly became clear that it no longer worked, at least as a business model.

About a year after starting publication, the *Long Beach Register* became a Sunday-only publication, distributed as a section inside the *Orange County Register* (Long Beach subscribers started getting the *OC Register*). By December 2014, they shut it down altogether. Kushner and his partner were gone by March 2015 and the *Register* was getting ready to be sold.

It should be noted that our newspaper chain had declared bankruptcy in 2010 and had been purchased by Alden Global Capital, a Wall Street hedge fund. In 2015, Alden created the Digital First Media Corporation and bought the *Register* along with the rest of Freedom Communications, making it the third largest media company in the country.

CHAPTER 57

So we won the newspaper war. Digital First handed out awards the following year.

They gave me National Weekly Editor of the Year, and named *Press-Telegram* editor Melissa Evans Small Daily Editor of the Year. I think I still have the plaque somewhere.

Chapter 58

Even off by myself at a convention in St. Paul, Minnesota, to pick up that award, I had no desire to drink. After the awards dinner, I went back up to my room despite attempts to coax me into staying for the after-dinner party.

I had been sober for 13 or 14 years by then. I confess, I no longer regularly attended AA meetings, even though I believed in the Twelve Steps and the mantra of working the program because it works.

I even acted as a sponsor for a friend or two trying to get sober.

So instead of saying I didn't think I needed meetings, I used the excuse that I had gotten too busy. The smaller newsroom gave me more to do, and I was working 60 or 70 hours a week. I served on a bunch of boards. Busy, busy, busy.

The fact is, I really didn't think I needed the meetings, and I didn't want to tell all the old-timers that. It sounds corny, and more than a little egotistic, but I had been touched by God.

One of the many things I keep from the AA program is the Serenity Prayer. It is prayed at every meeting, and I pray it twice every day; when I get up and when I go to bed. I use the short version. It goes like this:

"Dear God, Grant me the serenity to accept the things I cannot change, the courage to change the things I can, and the wisdom to know the difference."

Those 28 words, an iteration of a prayer by American theologian Reinhold Niebuhr, pack quite a punch. I know they hold teachings I need to work on every day.

That first phrase – accept the things I cannot change – is all

CHAPTER 58

about giving control to God and understanding I am not in control. That is a very difficult concept for a control freak like me. I'm supposed to be able to fix anything, right?

Wrong. That's God's job.

Still, there are things I am supposed to do something about – the courage to change the things I can. Working for the betterment of my community and to help my neighbors is something I think God wants me to do, especially if I can sneak in a word or two about Him.

Figuring out which is which is often beyond me. That's the point of the prayer, isn't it? I need God's help to figure it out – to give me the wisdom to know the difference.

I leaned on the concepts of community and accountability too, just like I learned in the AA meetings. I just used the church to fill that role.

Specifically, I used a men's Bible study group. It started around 2003 or 2004, and I'm still going to the same group today, 20-some-years later.

We did study books of the Bible or books about concepts taught there. But it also quickly became an accountability group. We talked about troubles we were facing, decisions we had to make, occasionally even the good things that happened to us.

The group size fluctuated between four and eight guys for a long time. Some would come and go. There are still two of us from the original group attending. He is my close friend, and often my conscience.

As we grew, the emphasis slowly shifted to more study and less accountability talk. Too many family stories had left too little time to talk about God.

But I can and do still talk to a couple of the guys about how we're doing on trying to follow God's path. They are a blessing to me. I hope I let them know that.

They help me with the wisdom to know the difference, too.

Chapter 59

I don't mean to make it sound like my faith journey was easy, or simple. I was born again in a conservative church in the Grace Brethren (now Charis) denomination. And I grew up in the very liberal 1960s and 1970s.

I was all about the scientific method, and evolution was the Gospel truth (sorry) in my high school and college classes. Now I found myself in a congregation that believed the Bible was the literal truth.

I had spent most of my career either being the most liberal person in a conservative group or the most conservative person in a liberal group – the Chamber of Commerce board and the Arts Council board, for example. Admittedly, it took some time, but I learned to (at least mostly) keep quiet when the Word was the topic of discussion.

I'm sure I am not the only one who struggles with hard concepts like God allowing the death of children.

Why is evil allowed in the world? Why do the bad guys win, at least part of the time? Where is the justice?

Each of those questions touched off weeks, sometimes months of debate and discussion, with my fellow Christians and with myself. I haven't totally come around to some of the theologians' explanations.

We did totally agree on the basics, though. Jesus was my savior. He had died for my sins.

I had been saved by the grace of God. I knew that, because I had a personal relationship with Him.

God's Holy Spirit dwells in me, helps me do the right things at the right time.

CHAPTER 59

I live with God.

I hasten to add that that doesn't mean I do nothing but focus on religion. Quite the contrary. I don't spend nearly enough time praying or reading.

Most of the nonprofit organizations I volunteer with have a faith component, but not all. I donate faithfully to my church, but it isn't the 10% tithe many churches require. Adding in the donations to the nonprofits gets it closer, but still not 10%.

My excuse, beyond being a newspaper guy, was and is what I saw as a Biblical imperative to support my family first and foremost. I was essentially the sole income. The kids had flown the coop (John joined the Marines out of high school), but there were still weddings for both girls, then grandkids, and so on.

That was sort of a reason for not giving money to panhandlers on the street, too. It was a charge from Jesus to care for those less fortunate than ourselves, I know, but I convinced myself that giving street people money just enabled their problem or addiction.

I've fought with that conflict for a long time. I have been involved in the efforts to alleviate, if not end, homelessness for decades – remember, I sat on a task force during Beverly O'Neill's tenure charged with finding a way to "End Homelessness in 10 Years." I got quite the education about the realities of the homeless population.

I wrote many stories and columns about components of homelessness. I was in the middle of debates about the proper approach to alleviate homelessness. Precious Lamb Preschool deals solely with homeless children, and I did all I could to help them. I volunteered as a board member of a housing and service facility for homeless military veterans. I went on homeless counts for the city.

But I have almost never interacted with an actual homeless street person. I am embarrassed to say that. It's just not something I want to do. I honestly don't think I can do it.

Not much of a newspaperman there. It's still a reason I question how I can call myself a Christian.

Help me with that, God. Please?

Chapter 60

After the marriage of the *Grunion* and the *Press Telegram* to defeat the *Register's* run at Long Beach, there was no going back. I started attending the Southern California News Group's editorial meetings. There were requests from *P-T* editors for *Grunion* staffers to handle stories.

We crossed the Rubicon when *Grunion*-written stories began appearing in the *P-T* before the *Grunion* came out on Thursday.

Here's a pretty good example of the corporate takeover.

Simon had hired two young sports writers who had become experts in prep sports while working for a young internet outlet called the *Long Beach Post*. Mike Guardabascio and JJ Fiddler dominated the coverage – so much so that we started a full sports section in August 2011. We even sent Mike and JJ to England to cover the 2012 London Summer Olympics. Simon, who grew up near London, had connections to make it happen.

After the newspaper war, there were some fairly tense conversations about whether the sports stories they generated for us could appear in the *P-T*. The corporate argument was that they owned the *Grunion*, so they owned what appeared in the *Grunion*. We argued back that Mike and JJ were contract employees and had control over where their content appeared.

We kept control for a bit. Then the *P-T* made Mike and JJ an offer they couldn't refuse – fulltime jobs, with benefits. And we kept our section, thanks to the Sports Guys' loyalty.

In the meantime, our reporting staff continued to shrink. Thank God I had a few good freelancers and columnists. And I kept control of the editorial content through the layout process.

Now we are back to when Alden Global Capital, primarily a

CHAPTER 60

hedge fund, had taken total control over Digital Media First and Tribune Publishing. They and a few other large owners controlled almost all print media in the country. Most of the big chains went public, selling stock.

That's important because newspaper people no longer had much control over the fate of newspapers. It became all about the bottom line, with profit margins the measuring stick of success.

Bad news came from the local and state management – no raises, cuts to staff, etc. I felt sorry for them. They were all newsmen and newswomen to the core. They fit the cliche of ink in their veins, and I stood by them.

But they had to follow the edicts from the higher-ups, even when they knew it was bad for the newspaper and bad for the public.

Which brings us back to the Sports Guys. In a radical shift for many local dailies in the chain, a new model of less local news and prep sports was rolled out for 2018 to allow for more consolidation. Mike and JJ were laid off after they declined positions that had little or nothing to do with prep sports.

In a move that was brave if not overly business-savvy, the pair launched a nonprofit sports website called The562.org focusing exclusively on Long Beach athletes. They kept their contract with the *Grunion* to continue the sports section and to bring in some needed cash.

Their nonprofit online-only approach became more and more common over time, with national (*ProPublica*), state (*CalMatters*) and local (*Long Beach Post*) outlets all relying on donors to keep the doors open. To their credit, The562.org is still alive and thriving today.

Postscript: The less local, no prep sports experiment lasted less than a year. Many subscribers dropped the *P-T*, saying they took it primarily for prep sports. That segment of coverage was back in 2019, without Mike and JJ.

Chapter 61

I think I can say without fear of contradiction that 2020 was a very bad year.

When the COVID-19 pandemic hit America in March that year, it spread like a wildfire. (A cliche, but true.) There was no cure, very little treatment available and a high mortality rate for those who caught the disease.

I wrote some very sad stories that year. The virus was so contagious that hospital wings were sealed off. People watched parents and grandparents – older people were very susceptible to the disease – go into closed intensive care rooms to die alone.

There were uplifting stories too. Those featured people, often students, doing what they could to make life easier for those suffering from COVID.

Efforts to slow the spread came quickly. Schools were closed. Offices, including ours, closed as well. There were runs on grocery and big-box stores for everything from toilet paper to soup as the supply chain fell apart.

Technology quickly became king, led by a thing called Zoom. The group video chat app allowed teachers to connect with their students, at least those with a computer and an internet connection. It was an inefficient and less than effective teaching tool, but it was better than nothing.

By mid-2020, pretty much everything that could be done by computer was being done that way. It was called working remotely.

That didn't count all the nurses, doctors, grocery clerks, mail carriers, airplane pilots and all the others whose jobs required in-person contact. We called them heroes, and that's what they were.

CHAPTER 61

We at the *Grunion* had been gradually headed for electronic production before the pandemic. Our pages were put together on the computer, digitized and sent to the printer by computer. I had been receiving most of the columns and stories from outside writers via email.

Scientists worked feverishly to come up with a vaccine to stop the disease, but still weren't totally certain how it spread and how contagious it was. Almost all events were canceled, and stores that were open required people to stand six feet apart.

Attending church was actually controversial. Crowds congregating inside had been banned, and only the most radical priests and pastors defied that edict.

Our church started with remote services broadcast on Facebook and YouTube, then gradually transitioned to one or two services conducted on the church lawn – being outdoors with air circulating was supposed to be safer, especially when you were wearing a mask.

Maria and I put our camp chairs to good use. In some ways, the outdoor services felt even more powerful than those in the sanctuary. It wasn't the Sermon on the Mount, but...

I was a little surprised at how quickly we adjusted to putting out a newspaper with all of us sitting at computer terminals at home. Our production guys were real wizards at the graphics involved.

The biggest issue was finding enough photographs to make the paper look decent. I had a brave freelance photographer or two as well as writers willing to go out and get close enough to get the picture. I'll admit to doing some of that myself.

All of the papers were operating much the same as us. Offices became mail drops, if that.

And this, in my mind, put more than a few nails in the newspaper coffin.

Chapter 62

We proved that we could produce a newspaper (and a website) without an office. There had been talk before the pandemic of the backpack reporter — someone with a laptop able to file stories from the field or their home — but that was the exception, not the rule.

Now it was the real deal, for reporters, editors and more. Thanks to advances in computer programs and some pretty savvy production folks, the printer got everything needed to deliver a printed paper, all through the internet.

Zoom and Microsoft's equivalent, Teams, allowed for face-to-face (sort of) communication between editors and reporters, reporters and sources, etc. In Long Beach and elsewhere, city councils met virtually, including ways for the public to comment (those were pretty clunky).

Sounds pretty 21st Century, doesn't it? And it was. If COVID had struck even a decade earlier, I'm not sure how it would have worked out.

But. And there's always a But.

When Alden Capital and the other corporate types realized they could get papers produced without a physical office for editorial and advertising staff, a new source of revenue was realized — real estate.

In some places, buildings that had been owned were sold. In others, like the *Grunion's* office in the middle of Belmont Shore, long-term leases were dropped. In both cases, that was a pretty penny into corporate coffers. A one-time profit, to be sure, but a profit all the same.

I felt like we were saying community involvement be damned.

CHAPTER 62

People no longer had a place to go to complain about a story, to place a classified ad, to drop off a press release or to pick up a past edition.

Without that physical presence, it was much harder to convince people we were on their side. A letter to the editor? Email it. A news tip? Call the editor. What, you don't have his number?

There was a subtle shift in my mindset, too. I had a small office and pretty good Wi-Fi at my home, so I was functional. I have to admit, the dogs thought it was great to have someone around to give them mid-day snacks.

But I missed the camaraderie of an office with at least a few coworkers around. If I needed to bounce an idea off of Simon, the production guys, or a writer, I had to either put it in an email or hope that I could get them on the phone.

I fell victim more than once to the pity party of "it's all on me." God forgive me, but I occasionally took the stress out on Maria and/or the dogs with a snappish attitude.

And the cuts kept coming. A longtime friend and part-time proofreader didn't fit into the new all-remote workflow. I hated to tell him that.

That lack of proofreading, and often simple editing, can be seen in the declining quality of both print newspapers and online news outlets. I get embarrassed today when I see some of the silly errors that get put out there.

Chapter 63

When the corporate owners had sucked up all the real estate profit, they leaned on the internet technology again to find more "savings." By this time, post-COVID, stories had begun surfacing about work being outsourced.

There were complaints about pieces being done by centralized writing factories, with little to no local knowledge. It was a precursor to Artificial Intelligence.

As I've pointed out before, there is nothing that substitutes for boots on the ground, at least when it comes to community news. I've always lived in the towns I wrote about. I'm invested. I have ownership.

But that costs money, and the powers that be worked hard to get by with as little expense as they could.

So imagine the excitement when they found out they could outsource all that production stuff – the graphic details of putting a newspaper together before it goes to the printer.

In the case of the Southern California News Group, the outfit they discovered was in the Philippines. They started with the *Press Telegram* and other full-sized papers in the local chain – what the Philippine firm was set up to produce.

We hung on to our production guys for about six months, until the wrinkles of putting a tabloid-sized (think magazine) newspaper together was figured out with the Filipino company. Then the *Grunion* and the other weeklies were swallowed up.

I know this is pretty newspaper geek stuff, but it really does matter. Beyond the "reduction in force" we continued to experience, quite a bit of the layout process was outsourced to the Philippines too.

CHAPTER 63

In other words, I had less editorial control. I could say what went on the front page, and I could prioritize the rest of the stories, but I couldn't say what went where. And they wrote most of the headlines so they would fit the space allocated.

That made a difference, at least to me. There was a method to my madness when I put the sailing column on a page opposite a story about marina construction. Most of the time it wasn't that clear, but I took pride in the entire product, not just the front page.

I could and did ask for changes when they left out a story I thought was important, and they were unfailingly polite and ready to do what I wanted. But I couldn't ask my production guy what looked best where or if they could make a last-minute switch – they weren't there anymore.

Once again, I had less control over the *Grunion*, and I had to answer for the quality of the paper anyway.

It took away some of the joy.

Chapter 64

By this time, I was the only full-time editorial employee at the *Grunion*. I had some great columnists, the sports guys, a freelance photographer, and I was supposed to be using *Press-Telegram* stories.

Filling the *Grunion* wasn't really an issue. Filling it with the local news and people features I wanted our readers to have was more of a challenge.

I had started whining about working all the time on stuff I didn't really have much fun doing. In reality, I still made time for several nonprofits. I had been asked a few years back to join the Salvation Army board, so had added that to the list.

Then in 2023, the local Salvation Army brass asked me to start an advisory board for the Salvation Army Adult Rehabilitation Center in Long Beach.

As you know, the Army long has had a relationship with alcohol recovery — thanks "Guys and Dolls" — and now has an entire branch dedicated to the Adult Rehabilitation Center (A.R.C.) program. Most territories have one or more centers.

It's basically the perfect storm for me. The ministry is strongly Christian. The recovery program is the Twelve Steps of Alcoholics Anonymous, expanded to include addiction to a number of drugs. Most of the applicants are either homeless or close to it.

And they needed someone who knew how an advisory board is supposed to work.

Long Beach's A.R.C. is for men only. There are facilities for women in nearby cities, and the Salvation Army structure made sure we were in close contact if a woman came to us needing help.

CHAPTER 64

The facility had been rebuilt the year before, and was sparkling. There were 100 beds, truly dedicated Salvation Army officers in charge and a talented, hard-working staff.

What they didn't have was a decent public awareness campaign – check another box for me – and a board to turn to that could help connect with that public.

So I went out and found a few great board members and we started to work. One thing about every Salvation Army officer and employee I've ever met – they listen, and they are always grateful for help. That was the case here.

I was able to make a few connections in the community for them, and other board members tapped their networks. We got posters on city buses, announcements in churches and a lot more.

Maybe most importantly, I got the strong impression that the captains and staff really liked the fact that they didn't have to do it all on their own anymore. Like many boards, we didn't do much, if any, of the real work. (We've served Thanksgiving breakfast twice as of this writing.) But our presence really uplifted the folk who did – do the work, that is.

And it made more than a little difference when I talked to the clients that I could say "I'm Harry, and I'm an alcoholic." Several of the board members could do the same thing.

I can't resist the chance to do a little name-dropping here. I've known Paul Williams for more than a decade. Yes, that Paul Williams, the song writer for The Carpenters, Barbra Streisand and more. He played Little Enos of "Smoky and The Bandit" fame, along with numerous other movie roles.

Paul also happens to be a legend in the world of recovery. He has more than 30 years of sobriety after riding booze and drugs to the top of the Hollywood party circuit. When Paul talks, addicts listen.

He is also a very generous person. When I asked him to speak at the first-ever Night of Hope fundraiser for the Long Beach A.R.C. in 2024, he not only did it for free, but donated to the cause.

I love the man.

Chapter 65

As the world emerged from the COVID pandemic, there was some slight hope that the newspaper world would recover, at least a bit. No such luck.

We didn't have an office to go back to, even if we wanted to. I'm talking about the *Press-Telegram* and others in our chain as well as the *Grunion*.

It wasn't just Alden Capital-owned publications, either. At the *Los Angeles Times*, where there had been some hope after billionaire doctor Patrick Soon-Shiong bought it in 2018, there had been two buyouts to cut staff.

We were enduring a president who called mainstream media "the enemy of the people" and "fake news." Donald Trump made up his own "facts" in an alternative reality that had little connection to where most of us lived.

I was blessed with the focus on Long Beach and the credibility that 30 years of reporting on the same city gave me. And Trump's crew didn't have a bone to pick specifically with Long Beach. California was a different story.

I have to admit, though, that I was tiring. The stress of not being able to rely on a staff and the 60 or 70 hours of seven-day-a-week work started to get to me.

Maria was more than a little upset by my constant busyness, and that was compounded by the time I spent on my nonprofits. The working from home thing actually helped that a bit, since we were at least in the same building.

But walking out of my office and declaring "Honey, I'm home" as I walked into the living room got old quickly. She only smiled the first few times I said it.

CHAPTER 65

She got away from the drag by going down to San Marcos to take care of two of our grandchildren every other week. An occasional multiple-week visit to her sister living in Las Vegas helped her mood, too.

When she was gone, that just gave me more time to work. The dogs had beds in the office, so they were happy as long as I got up and gave them a treat once in a while.

God continued to provide, and even though we were essentially still living paycheck to paycheck, we were in a lot better shape than a lot of people. And for a change, I got a break from the economy at large.

Thanks to the ultra-low mortgage rate coming out of the pandemic, I was able to refinance the house. I took out enough money to pay off all the credit cards and one of the cars. It was a blessing indeed.

Now if I could just stop whining about working so much. It wasn't making an impression with my friends anymore.

Does the phrase "you made your own bed" sound familiar?

Chapter 66

There are times when a transition seems inevitable. Then there are times when it takes a while to catch on to the fact that God is opening a door.

Over the years, God has had to take a 2x4 to my head fairly often in order to get my attention and shift direction. A DUI arrest, a heart attack, that sort of thing.

This was more subtle.

A long-time friend of mine had made the move from the public sector to private business after a couple of decades climbing the government ladder. There was an opportunity at his new company for a little writing – profiles of young entrepreneurs, to be exact.

We struck a deal for me to do some freelance work for him. Maria was not happy about still more work until she heard how much they would pay me for each story.

So I added one more task. It was actually fun, talking to these extremely smart, excited young people about starting businesses no one had heard of before.

I only did one or two stories a month. But I learned a lot.

That went on for most of a year.

The *Grunion* staff box had shrunk to three full-time people – me, Publisher Simon and Ad Executive Jonathan. Still, the *Grunion* actually placed third statewide for best small weekly at the end of that year.

My friend/client for freelance articles knew about the broader newspaper crisis generally and the *Grunion's* lack of resources specifically. He also knew I was 69 years old with a bad heart.

So he made me an offer – a very good offer – for a full-time job. Except I had a hard time accepting it.

CHAPTER 66

I wasn't sure I could give up the *Grunion* and the work I did there. What would happen to the paper? What would happen to the city?

How would they ever get along without me?

Actually, the issue was that I loved being in the middle of things. I had 40 years of the adrenaline rush of chasing a good story, an important story. And admit it, I really liked people thinking I made a difference by writing.

So I began praying. I asked my men's Bible study group what I should do, and asked for their prayers. I talked to Maria. A lot.

Bless her, she didn't out and out tell me what to do. But she did point out I'd still be making a difference with my work with the nonprofits – I'd even have more time for them.

Maria only played the "it will be good for you" card once. She reminded me of my increasing unhappiness and frustration with the lack of resources. The stress, the long hours, the heart condition were left unsaid, but still there.

I did the pro-and-con thing. The money was significantly, very significantly, better. I'd be working 8 hours a day, and the amount of time off was almost unbelievable.

The last time I had taken a full week off, it was for open heart surgery and recovery. I was depriving Maria of vacations most people thought of as a given.

We Christians like to talk a lot about how when one door closes, God opens another. In this case the first door was still open, but God offered an alternative. Was I supposed to walk through the new door?

I concluded I was – supposed to walk through the door, that is. And wonder of wonders, the senior editor for all of SCNG wanted me to keep writing my "A Pinch of Salt" column. I would still have a voice in the paper.

I gave up the executive editor position on March 1, 2023 – exactly 31 years after taking the job.

Chapter 67

I made the announcement in my column two weeks before the departure. It sparked a round of parties and a period of nonprofits honoring me with awards at their galas.

I kept emphasizing that I wasn't going anywhere. I protested that I would still be writing the column, and remain just as involved in all my causes as I had been. I would continue to attend events, both political and charitable.

But I didn't answer the phone with "this is the *Grunion*," and all the To The Editor emails went elsewhere, at least most of the time. I was more than a little lost.

Here's where it made the biggest difference. Just more than a month after I had started the new job, we had a week in Hawaii scheduled – I bought it at a live auction for one of my favorite charities.

The new company sent me off with their blessing. I took my computer along, of course, and started checking emails when we got settled in the Honolulu condo. This despite Maria's glare. But that's what I had been doing forever, and thought it was expected.

Then the CEO's executive assistant, who doubled as the HR person, replied to one of my replies to her email.

"Thank you," she said. "Now stop it. No more emails. You are on vacation."

She made a lifetime friend in Maria on the spot.

I had some trouble adjusting to writing for the private sector. There was still the research, and the structure of writing is pretty universal.

But I wasn't supposed to be writing balanced pieces. I was supposed to show how good the company was at its job, and why

CHAPTER 67

the reader wanted to come on board in one way or another.

This is/was a financial services/investment company, which means it is regulated by the SEC, FINRA and a couple other acronyms. That oversight includes communications, which means there is a compliance officer to make sure I didn't cross any lines.

"But I attributed it," I would exclaim. "That's what he said. What do you mean I can't say that?"

It would take another book to explain all the ins and outs of compliance. Lots of talented people make a living telling companies how they must comply with all the rules and regulations. That included telling me what to do.

I wasn't in Newspaperland anymore. And it took some adjusting to realize people could actually tell me what to write and what not to write in this brave new world.

There were tradeoffs. The CEO who hired me and for whom I wrote most frequently was a Christian. Our philosophies aligned – do the best you can, help others, make the world (the community) a better place.

That meant I was writing what I believed a good 90% of the time.

And I really did have more time to help a pretty wide range of charities, large and small. I started going to two Bible studies a week and got involved with a couple of committees at church as well.

I had time to spend with Maria, grandkids and the rest of the family. Just as important, maybe more so, I was/am really with them instead of worrying about that big story I still had to write.

I decided I went through the door God wanted me to go through.

Chapter 68

I began feeling my age in 2024. It wasn't so much that I was physically slowing down – that was a given.

Instead, I was shaken by the deaths of several of my peers. Four men in particular who I had long relationships with passed that year. Two were after long illnesses while two were sudden and unexpected.

Two of the four were in our men's Bible study group, which met and still meets at 6 a.m. on Friday. Both were Godly, gentle men.

I've avoided using names where possible in this book, but I feel compelled to tell you the story of Lee Howell. Lee was my age, but he was a much more mature Christian. He was the epitome of a gentle giant – 6 feet 7 inches of love and caring.

When his doctors found a tumor in his brain, he took it stoically. It was all part of God's plan. At least as far as I could see, he quietly acquiesced with the treatments doctors prescribed – primarily to keep giving his wife and children hope and as much time as possible together.

That included experimental treatments with attachments on his head – something else for Lee to smile at quietly.

Speaking of quiet, he seldom talked of his faith, but it was clear in his attitude. The phrase God's plan was real for Lee, and he was proof of that power by just being Lee.

As the tumor progressed and limited Lee's ability to speak, he would sit smiling, listening to us debate the nuances of Scripture. He made it clear he enjoyed the companionship of Christian friends trying to learn more about God.

He wasn't trying to, but Lee taught me a lot about living with God. The quiet acceptance of God's will, the visible anticipation of going to meet Jesus was embodied in him.

I suspect we all cried when he died. We were crying for ourselves and his family, not him. He was where he wanted to be.

The deaths of two other friends were far less comfortable. One sat down in his chair for a nap and never woke up. The other wasn't feeling well, so he decided to lie down for a bit. He never got up.

Both were older than me, but I thought they were both in better health than me. Their sudden passing made it clear that God could take any of us at any time. If you weren't right with Him, you were risking never being able to get right with Him.

I was honored to be asked to emcee my golf buddy's Celebration of Life – no memorial allowed. It was a big affair (he was a well-known and important city leader), and secular in nature.

I knew pretty much everyone involved in the program, including his wife. She was/is a good friend.

With her permission, I added a prayer to my introduction, and a blessing to the conclusion.

From the response, I have to say that God's presence worked out pretty well.

Chapter 69

As we entered the home stretch for Christmas 2024, I thought I was done with deaths for the year.

That wasn't God's plan.

I have a sister a little more than a year younger than I am. We haven't been estranged exactly, but we rarely had contact.

She had split from our family shortly after high school (she was pregnant) and moved to the Deep South with the child's father. I was busy going out on my own young adult life, and we barely acknowledged birthdays and Christmas.

We crossed paths over the years – my grandmother's 80th birthday, Dad's second marriage – but it was brief and not always pleasant.

It had gotten a bit better in the last decade or so, with phone calls at Thanksgiving, etc. I didn't really try to keep track of her personal life, though.

Then in the late summer, her son called to tell me she had been in a car accident and wasn't doing too well. She was suffering from dementia and her internal organs were starting to fail.

There were a couple of check-ins, but she didn't seem to get worse or better. The year went on.

Then, on Dec. 8, I got a call. "She passed last night," he said.

Over the next few days, there was some back and forth about what to do. She had wanted to be buried, but none of the family had made any arrangements before she died. It was clear they didn't have the money to do anything now, either.

I am the oldest brother. My younger brother wasn't in the position to help.

The son and I compromised on the arrangements; cremation

CHAPTER 69

followed by a burial. That was half the cost of a full-body funeral.

I paid for it. It was the right thing to do.

A private funeral was set up for Dec. 22 in Nashville, Tenn. The family had lived near there when the kids were kids, and they knew a pastor there. I booked a red-eye and a one-night hotel stay.

That afternoon, we gathered at the cemetery. There were six of us – her son, her daughter, her granddaughter and great-granddaughter, me and the pastor. It was around freezing when we began.

The pastor offered a few words and a good prayer. Then the urn was lowered into a small hole in the ground and it was done.

But I was able to talk to both the son and the daughter about Jesus and their mother's professed faith. I'm not sure I could have done that without the Celebration of Life experience earlier that year.

I did it though. With God's help.

Maybe that's what He had planned for me. Maybe that's why He had me go through what I have gone through in this life.

I know it was a God thing.

Epilogue

Thank you so much for listening to my story.

Newspapers still haven't faded completely away, and there are dedicated journalists continuing to fight the good fight, acting as watchdogs, truth tellers and information sources. It's a real fight right now, with real consequences. I'm on their side.

There still are plenty of alcoholics and addicts out there. I'm an alcoholic, but a recovering one. My last drink was on September 13, 2001, and I have every intention of keeping it that way.

I'm also committed to helping other alcoholics and addicts find the peace of sobriety in God's house. Corny? Maybe. But I believe it can be.

I know I am a sinner, saved only through the grace of God. No matter how hard I work (and you know I'm going to work hard), my ultimate salvation is up to Him.

As I hope you can see now, it is indeed a God thing.

Thank you, God.

March 1, 2025 – Harry Saltzgaver

Acknowledgements

There are many, many people who have played a role in this story. I want to thank each and every one of them, but space prohibits. Please allow me to thank a few here.

Start with Steve Haynes, the man who taught me newspapering. I was blessed with other strong editors and bosses, but Steve's the one who gave me the foundation.

John and Fran Blowitz took a chance on me with their baby, the *Grunion Gazette*. They stuck with me through some bad times, and allowed me the freedom to become a part of Long Beach.

John Lowe kindly spent his time and expertise to improve the words. He is a member of the church, which is my rock.

Then there's Maria. 25 years of love and support. I love you.

Most of all, there's God. He has all the power, and all the glory. Thank you, God.